sparks

Inspiration for Extinguishing the
Power of Fear and Igniting
Amusement, Knowing, and Trust

emily souder, LCSW-C

Copyright © 2020 Emily Souder

All rights reserved. No portion of this book may be reproduced in any form without permission from the publisher, except as permitted by U.S. copyright law. For permissions contact: nestingspacellc@gmail.com

Visit the author's website at www.nestingspacellc.com.

Cover & interior design by Jess Creatives
Edited by Jodi Brandon Editorial

ISBN: 978-1-7346309-0-9

This guide is not meant as a replacement for psychotherapy or working through mental wellness topics with a professional. The reader should consult a physician or a mental health professional in matters relating to his/her mental health and particularly with respect to any symptoms that may require diagnosis or medical attention.

First Edition

Dedication

To W & L:

Keep those fires lit. I love you with all my heart.
Thank you for inspiring me every day!

Acknowledgments

There is no way that my creativity would burst into book form without tremendous support. I am so very grateful for the support provided to me by my husband, who listens (mostly tirelessly) to my ideas and frustrations; my kiddos, who inspired me at every turn; my family and friends, who helped with the kids and provided listening ears; my beta readers (Lily and Val—thank you, thank you for taking time out of your busy lives to read my work and provide honest feedback); my dear sister and other friends who read or skimmed; my editor, Jodi, who brings all the knowledge and also tons of fun; and my designer, Jess, whose work paired impeccably with my vision. I could not have done this alone, and I am so thankful for my team!

contents

Introduction 9
Part One: Fear 13
    Chapter 1: Fear and its Flavors 15
    Chapter 2: The Roots of My Fear 23
    Chapter 3: Anxiety as Fear/Fear as Anxiety 25
    Chapter 4: Slow Down 29
    Chapter 5: Reiki 33
    Chapter 6: Health Scares 35
    Chapter 7: Holding Back: What's Poop Got to Do with It? ... 37
    Chapter 8: How Fear Protects Us 39
    Chapter 9: Do the Work; Do it Anyway 41
    Chapter 10: Filter out the Fear-Based Crud 43
    Chapter 11: What They Think Is . . . What They Think 45
    Chapter 12: What's under the Fear? 47
    Chapter 13: Setting the Intention to Release Fear 49
Part Two: Amusement 51
    Chapter 14: Lighting Your Fire 55
    Chapter 15: Meeting Amusement 57
    Chapter 16: Share Your Fears, Increase Amusement and Trust 59
    Chapter 17: Finding Amusement in the Splatter 61
    Chapter 18: Life Is Messy 63
    Chapter 19: Bark in My Teeth 65
    Chapter 20: Sing It 67
    Chapter 21: Deep Joy 69
    Chapter 22: Snuggles 71
    Chapter 23: Bone Broth and Ice Cream 73
    Chapter 24: One of These Things Is Not Like the Other
        (and That's Okay) 75

Chapter 25: You Broke an Axle 77

Chapter 26: Mini Meditations 79

Chapter 27: "I Believe in You, but I'm Not Afraid of You" 83

Chapter 28: Gratitude 85

Part Three: Knowing, Trust, and Other Fun 87

Chapter 29: Intuition and Knowing 89

Chapter 30: Owning My Knowing 91

Chapter 31: Using Your Knowing to Meet Your Inner Child 95

Chapter 32: Trust 99

Chapter 33: Releasing Doubt and Trusting Yourself 101

Chapter 34: Leaning into Trust and Taking Your Time 103

Chapter 35: Compassion 105

Chapter 36: Authenticity and Self-Care 107

Chapter 37: Generosity 109

Chapter 38: The Only Way in Is In 111

Chapter 39: Well, That's Funny 113

Conclusion 115

Resources 117

About the Author 120

INTRODUCTION

I am no stranger to fear. And really, are any of us? Fear found me at an early age, by nature or nurture, or a bit of both. I was often puzzled by it, unmoored by it. It felt like something I couldn't escape. For many years it manifested as anxiety and self-doubt. It took years of work and learning, experimenting and growing, to start to see that life wouldn't be that way forever. Even once I learned that lesson, I continue to learn it again and again, subject as most of us are to almost an amnesia of having gotten through hard things before. Once I began deepening my education (through both day-to-day life and schooling) and spiritual practice, I started learning about things that existed on the other side of fear. And the only way to get to those things was—you guessed it—by going through.

Moving through fear is scary, but that's not all. It's also empowering, motivating, and incredible. It gives way to so many things we couldn't imagine. Working with our fears rather than against them gives us a whole new set of options we couldn't possibly see before. Rather than shutting down and pushing away possibilities for ourselves that scare us, we can choose ways to make them a reality. And there are countless ways to do that!

When my husband and I were dating, he started referring to a spark that he felt between us. At some point, it became a nickname for me: Sparky, which at times shortens to Sparks, depending on my husband's mood. It's usually very playful. It felt so fitting to use here, to honor the energy that I wanted to share with you! I enjoy lighting people up. It feels good. Lighting others up lights *me* up. What better way to light the way than through fear and into something else? As dark as that tunnel feels, let me be a source of brightness along the way.

When I was younger, I focused way too much on the external validation I got from others' reactions to how I acted or how I appeared to be. I was heavily impacted by the climate of the emotions around me, and I didn't value the importance of keeping my own fire lit—just for me—before sharing it with others or having it reflect someone else's passion. I learned over time (and am still learning) how to tune into the state of my fire to not let it extinguish.

One of the things that kept my inner flame from developing into a beautiful, healthy fire was fear. Fear, something I gave quite a bit of attention to during those early years and beyond, spritzed water on my flame. Fear taunted my inner fire and made it feel small, like it could never be the bonfire that it dreamed of becoming.

Amusement, a concept I came to see in a new way while deepening my spiritual practices, helped take what I was learning about moving away from fear and elevate it to a whole new level. Amusement (or lighthearted entertainment, as I like to think of it) encouraged me to open up and fuel my fire with confidence. It was one of many important pieces that came together to help me move forward with the practice of shedding fear.

Learning through living all life has to offer has contributed to this shedding process. I paid for some of the experiences, and others were given to me freely. The free experiences were no less valuable in contributing to this shedding of fear. Becoming a mother, being married, having challenges with anxiety and depression, starting my own business—all of these "free" lessons (just because no money was paid, certainly there were costs) were opportunities to grow. As you will see in the coming pages, fear gives us a chance to become bigger, better versions of ourselves, but only if we lean into the opening.

A couple other concepts felt particularly relevant to include in this book. I felt called to dive into an exploration of the subjects of trust and intuition (which I refer to as knowing) as they relate to releasing the power of fear. With trust, we start to experiment with letting go of control, knowing things will turn out okay in the end. With our inner knowing, we turn some of that trust toward ourselves and what our "gut feeling" tells us is true.

This book is my invitation to you to view things differently by digging in and becoming aware of and familiar with your fear, and by starting to think of how life might look with fear being less powerful. Maybe you've never considered the presence of amusement, trust, and knowing in your life before—whether they're there, whether they're tiny or huge. These might be completely new concepts. How exciting! Hang in there with me as we explore, and perhaps what follows are some sparks I can share with you.

PART ONE
FEAR

"The natural ups and downs of life can either generate personal growth or create personal fears."
~ Michael A. Singer, *The Untethered Soul*

Fear is a natural part of our inner landscape. It's an expected part of being human and experiencing the life we are living. We all have a history with fear. It's something we have in common, and yet the sources of it can vary so much from person to person.

I haven't "made it." I haven't reached some endpoint of conquering fear and standing on the other side. I don't believe there is such a destination! I am on this journey *with* you. What I have learned to do is become very, very aware of fear. Mostly, I don't let it drive the bus (or the train, or the car, or the boat). But I'm human, and there are days when it still gets the best of me. Because I don't know about you, but I'm always a little suspicious when people aren't transparent about their very human struggles. Ups-and-downs, ins-and-outs, and around-and-arounds are real. Even if you've been a superstar mountain climber for years and years, I'm sure there are days when it still feels hard.

I never imagined in my wildest dreams that I would have changed my relationship to fear so much from when I was young. There were times when I felt I would be stuck in the fear vortex forever. But here I am, countless hours of life later. Ironically, it feels a bit scary to say out loud that I don't feel as controlled by fear. What could be next? What the hell will jump out from behind my bathroom door while I'm brushing my teeth tomorrow morning? You know what? *It doesn't matter.*

It doesn't matter because those things that my mind will create are all made up anyway. Those possibilities are my mind's way of trying to prepare me for the certainly uncertain future, but it's a place where my mind is falling short. We get into this more later, but often we rely on protective behaviors and thoughts long after they stop effectively serving us. There are ways to release these behaviors and thoughts, and we look into that as well.

We have a choice about how we react to what life tosses our way. Many times we have an initial knee-jerk reaction, but if we can pause, tune in, and slow down, we find that we have more options than we first thought. The only option is no longer to just run and hide, but maybe to confront the feeling, even if it's uncomfortable. Discomfort can awake fear like no other.

If we decide not to run, fear invites us to grow. It leaves an opening for us to challenge everything it has encouraged us to believe about ourselves and what is possible for us. If we don't go beyond the knee-jerk reaction, we never get that chance. As humans, we tend to recoil from pain or even the potential of it, for sure. But what if the pain was worth it? What if the pain leads to the birth of a new version of yourself who can navigate this life with courage, bravery, and grace?

These invitations for growth need not always be huge, life-changing ones. For example, let's pretend you have an opportunity to attend a type of exercise class that you've never tried before. It scares you, and you wonder about whether your body is capable, what you will look like doing the moves, and what people will think of you. Your inner child who remembers how humiliating it is to be teased is telling you not to jump in. If you have the presence to be able to express compassion to that young child and tell her that she is safe and that you're going to try something new, there are tons of possibilities that could be revealed. Maybe you go to the class, have fun, or make new friends. Maybe you laugh at yourself, learn something new about your body, or gain a new passion. Or, worst case, you go and none of those things happen. But at least you leave with the knowing that you *tried*. You stretched outside of your comfort zone, and the practice of making that stretch is invaluable. You see, you will never leave empty handed, because you are learning to grow despite the voice of fear.

CHAPTER 1
FEAR AND ITS FLAVORS

According to Merriam-Webster.com, fear is "an unpleasant often strong emotion caused by anticipation or awareness of danger."

The definitions of *fear* I noted through some good old Internet exploration all seemed to agree on the unpleasant nature of fear. It feels icky. We want out. It's not a state we want to be in for very long. But let's not forget, there is a range of fear. The brand of fear associated with running for your life while being chased by an angry bear is a bit different than the fear associated with stepping up on a stage to give a talk in front of a ton of people for the first time. And yet . . .

And yet in the moment it is highly likely that, even if we aren't being chased by anything or our lives aren't in danger, our minds can misconstrue information to make us believe that something terrible is afoot.

I like the mention of the *anticipation* of danger. We don't know for sure that it's coming. But we *think* it might. We *worry* it might. We *fear* it might. As Jen Sincero writes in *You Are a Badass*, "The majority of the pain and suffering in our lives is caused by the unnecessary drama that we create." That *we* create. You and me. And I'm not even talking about the drama we create between ourselves and other people! I'm talking about the drama in our very own heads. The drama we create because we anticipate something that will probably not even occur. And yet we fear it. That's pretty powerful. That is the circus that our very own mind puts on.

The fear that I focus on in this book is not the running-from-a-bear fear, though. It's the day-to-day fear that lives in your head and keeps you from reaching your goals and living your fullest life. It's the one that keeps you small and fuels your self-doubt. I'm not an animal behaviorist and therefore know little about how to keep a bear from chasing you. But the thoughts in your head? Those I know something about. Through my education and working with clients over the years, I've become intimately familiar with thoughts. (Not to mention the ones in my own head. I know them better than the back of my hand.)

Flavors of Fear

Can you imagine if there was a fear ice cream shop? Or a cupcake shop? Oh my goodness. The selection of flavors of fear would be overwhelming. And some of them had better be gluten free.

We might think of fear as feeling one particular way in our bodies (electric, hot, pulsing, etc.), but what about the array of flavors of our fear thoughts? The number of ways fear can show up and hide behind other thoughts is staggering. Half the time we might not even know it's there because it's hidden *so* darn well. These are just some of the ways fear shows up:

- Fear of missing out
- Fear of failure
- Fear of embarrassment or humiliation
- Fear of not being accepted
- Fear of not being prepared
- Fear of the unknown
- Fear of something happening to us or to someone we love
- Fear of something not happening to us or to someone we love
- Fear of what others think

Do any of these come with hot fudge on top?

Let's dip into these a little deeper. I guarantee you that this list is not exhaustive; new and different flavors may occur to you. You will notice that some of these types overlap with each other, and that's okay. Some of these go hand in hand, like a double scoop on a gorgeous (or terrifying) ice cream cone.

Fear of Missing Out
Fear of missing out is exactly what it sounds like. When we feel this type of fear, we feel concerned that we are going to be left out of an important event or activity. The assumption, then, would be that not participating

would have negative ramifications—things like social isolation, jealousy, or not gaining something like a resource or experience. Basically, unpleasant feelings and experiences.

The fear of missing out is absolutely something that existed prior to the Internet and social media. But there seems to have been a sharp uptick in the intensity and frequency, because now we know *all* the things. When I was younger, I might have felt bummed or left out if I couldn't make it to a sleepover. One could argue that my imagination was more dangerous than social media as far as creating things I *may* have been missing out on, and I suppose that could be the case, but these days we see it all laid out before our eyes.

Fear of Failure
This is a giant of fear flavors. It has all the chunky add-ins, complicating the smoothness of the underlying flavor. This one subtype of fear could go in so many directions. Put plainly, it means we're afraid we won't make it, succeed, or be successful. In modern times, this usually isn't a life-or-death scenario, but sometimes it does carry heavier consequences. The point is that many times it *feels* as if there is something that large looming above us, but usually there's not.

Fear of Embarrassment or Humiliation
As a society, we are so very, very aware of what others think of us, and most of us care about it a great deal. As psychologist and speaker Dr. Michael Gervais said on the online show *Impact Theory*, "The greatest fear in modern times is what other people think. . . . Our job is to love others and not give a shit what they think of us." If we are so worried about what others think of us, being embarrassed or humiliated is something we aim to avoid at all costs. There could be an underlying message this triggers within us, such as "I am worthless," "I'm no good at anything," or even "I'm a failure." (Remember the fear of failure? That really is connected to so many things).

Fear of Not Being Accepted
Each of us wants to be accepted and loved for who we are—who we really,

truly are. Our authentic self is desperate for validation and hugs from the universe. Acceptance feels good, but from an evolutionary perspective, it makes sense that we would want to be accepted for our survival. If we were shunned from the group, survival wouldn't look so good for us. Being shunned in modern times isn't as directly linked to death (although there is some interesting research about loneliness and health outcomes; see the Resources for more information), but it *is* linked to loneliness and isolation.

Fear of Not Being Prepared
When you're about to take an exam or give a presentation, how much do you go over in your head what you will say, skimming your thoughts for things you might have missed and wanting it to be perfect? So many times. You might rehearse a conversation in your head 15 times prior to having it—and when you do have it, it likely won't play out as you imagined anyway! We want to be prepared and get it right. If we don't succeed at this, it could lead to embarrassment, failure, and more. See how linked these are? (If you're a person who is good at just winging it and don't have any of these thoughts, awesome! That isn't me.)

Fear of the Unknown
Fear of what's next. Fear of what we don't know. This is a *huge* one for the clients that I work with in a therapy setting. They want to know the outcome before deciding on a course of action. For example, they want to know ahead of time if a certain action—moving houses or not moving, for example—will make them happier. And naturally, most people want me to be able to tell them whether or not it will. (As social workers sometimes say, "Sorry. My magic wand (or in this case, my crystal ball) is broken.")

The not knowing can drive us crazy, and anxiety (read: fear) absolutely thrives on that. As noted, our mind wants to calculate things down to minute details so that it can ensure our survival and success. Without that information, things start to get a little wonky (is that a clinical term?) in the thought department.

Chapter 1

Fear of Something Happening to Us or to Someone We Love
While writing this book, I read Thich Naht Hanh's book *Fear*. In it, he addresses the fear of getting old and dying that we all have. We all know that it is something that we will find our way to eventually, but many of us push it away or ignore it. It can be scary: *What does death feel like? Will we be cared for? What happens after death (fear of the unknown)?* This fear of death and illness extends beyond us and to those we care about as well. If something happens to them, it could mean that we will be separated, or it might remind us of our own immortality.

When I talk about "something happening," though, it's not always as grave as an illness or death. It might just be tripping in front of the audience when you're on your way to give a presentation (humiliation) or being terrified that your partner will leave you for someone else (abandonment). With this type of fear, as with the others, there is a whole range of reasons for the fear existing in the first place and the seriousness of the potential outcome of which we are so afraid.

Fear of Something Not Happening to Us or to Someone We Love
The flip side of something happening to us or to someone we love, is something *not* happening to us or to someone we love. Not getting that amazing apartment across from the bagel shop. Not landing the job we really want. Our children not doing well in school. Just as we can become very wrapped up in what *could* happen, we are just as likely to imagine what *won't* happen.

Fear of What Others Think (Closely Tied to Embarrassment)
Oh, this one. *This one.* This drove me for so much of my life, and I feel as though waking up to it—*really* waking up to it—was a game-changer. I love the quote "What other people think of you is none of your business." (I wish I knew who said that first!) Because it's not.

This doesn't mean that we go around acting like assholes and doing whatever we feel like. It's possible to live as a compassionate human being *and* go about your life without worrying about who likes your purple pants or career choice.

Just this morning, I was chatting with my friend Carrie about this. As she was trimming my hair, we chatted about self-confidence, self-worth, and what it has to do what people think of you. Carrie has a background as a hair stylist, but she's also recently become a professional coach, and is a talented, curious, beautiful woman with a hunger for learning about herself and the world. Not unlike many of us, Carrie has challenges with being able to feel confident enough to speak up when she's uncomfortable. She might go along with a situation and sit with regret later. "Oh yes," I said. "I've been there. I found it had a lot to do with being worried about what other people thought about me."

You might wonder about the relationship between having negative thoughts about yourself and having thoughts about what others think. When we are worried about how someone will react to us, or what they will think of us when we do something, it's often because what we fear they think (even though it might not be what they *actually* think) mirrors something we are telling ourselves. Here's an example.

Say you're at happy hour with your friend after work. Your friend wants you to stay longer and have a second beer. You're happy with the one drink you've had, and you're ready to go home. She pushes a bit, and you give in. How will she look at you and what will she say if you don't have another drink? You might read her face as saying you're boring or lame. Whether or not she actually thinks those things is none of your business. What *is* your business is what that idea is igniting as far as fears about yourself.

I really am boring.

Am I fun to be around?

Just like the other flavors of fear, fear of what others think is a call for you to turn inward and ask, "What message do you have for me this time, fear?" Once you shine a light on the spot of fear or insecurity, it starts the process of fizzling and drying up.

What Do We Do with All of These?

Whoa. Those are a lot of types of fear. It's not necessary to get too caught up in which flavor you're experiencing, though it can be helpful to identify the general type if possible since knowing that can guide your thoughts toward the message the fear is carrying for you. For example, if you can identify that the fear you're feeling is about something happening to you (say, totally bombing it when you give a pitch in front of your boss), then you can dig a bit deeper. You can see the threads of fear of failure as well and wonder about what it would mean for you if such a thing happened. (Is your true fear about losing your job? Looking silly?) Keep lifting up the layers until you get to the core of your fear. A lot of times, at the core of our fears there are common themes. Many of us fear that we won't be safe, or we won't be loveable. What themes do you notice?

As we move on, we will discuss making the shift to seeing things differently—less through fear and more through other lenses like amusement and trust. When we are able to shift how we perceive the world around us, we don't get so caught up in the stories from our past. Instead, we can attend to what is really happening in the moment and be open to possibility. We miss so much of the present moment by being completely in our heads (read: thoughts)! Being out of your head and in the flow of experiencing your life lets you find your way more easily to joy, humor, connection with others, and connection with yourself. Through my personal stories as well as some guidance, my hope is to nudge you a bit in the direction of curiosity and experimentation.

Exercise Idea

Start jotting down core fear themes as you notice them. See if you can find threads that run throughout your concerns. Circle the ones that come up the most!

CHAPTER 2
THE ROOTS OF MY FEAR

Fear had a large presence in my life for so long I almost can't remember some of its roots. Except I can. And like we do with stories (or narratives) about ourselves and our lives, especially the less-than-pleasant ones, I latched on. I found so many darn things that were terrifying, and I made them mean that the world was an unsafe place. Germs. Fire (I realize the irony given the title of this book). Saddam Hussein (don't ask me how it came to pass, but about age 5 or 6 I was terrified that a bad guy would cross the sea to get me). People who looked different than I did. The natural order of things.

Not surprisingly, most of these memories formed when I was 6 or younger. And I was as impressionable as they came.

There was the time when I was walking through the lobby in our small-town library and saw a man who was missing a leg. His pants leg just hung there. My brain couldn't make sense of it. I can still see the safety pins placed unevenly on the cuff of the leg of the pants that had no leg. I had no idea as a young one that missing a limb was even a possibility. It hadn't occurred to me. And then, once I knew it was a thing, it *bothered* me. It scared me. Rather than seeing this as interesting or different, I was scared.

Then there was the *National Geographic*-style nature show about wild dogs that have so many litters of pups that the older ones end up eating the younger ones alive. Oh. My. Goodness. The terror. I swear I was in my late 20s before I stopped getting all the feels in my stomach when I thought about this.

And no one can forget the time in kindergarten when I washed my hands until they were raw because I had seen a television special on germs. I had to wear socks on my hands overnight to let Vaseline moisturize my poor chapped hands.

Sparks

Fortunately, as I aged into adolescence, and then young adulthood, and adulthood, rather than turning away from some of the ways our world is hurting, I turned toward them. I volunteered at a hospital when I was 15, playing with kids being treated for cancer and holding tiny babies in the NICU. In high school I was passionate about volunteering with a local nonprofit organization that worked with homeless shelters. Interestingly, for the most part, fear didn't touch me in those settings. (There was that one time a guy at a spaghetti dinner asked me, "Can we have seconds?" I totally heard, "Can we have sex?" and I all but ran away. I'm not even sure what flavor of fear *that* was. Luckily it was all figured out, the guy got another plate of pasta, and we all had a good laugh because, as he said, "There was only one other thing you could have thought I said.")

Fear didn't touch many of my actions, but inside my head it opened a full-blown amusement park. Roller coasters, a Tilt-A-Whirl, probably about seven carousels. As you've likely noted, I had always run a bit anxious, even as a child. But it wasn't long before anxiety started getting in the way of my daily life. It distracted me from school and doing things with friends. It made me question many of my actions and shrink from my potential. At the time, I didn't see anxiety for what it really was: fear.

CHAPTER 3
ANXIETY AS FEAR/FEAR AS ANXIETY

Through my early to mid-20s, *anxiety* was a buzzword for me. Even just thinking the word or daring to speak it triggered a big physical reaction for me (increased heart rate, sweaty palms, etc.). It felt like this untouchable, clinical thing that was bigger than me. I worked with a few different therapists, and I don't remember any of them breaking anxiety down to where I could understand it as fear, at its roots. Even in my social work clinical education, I don't recall discussion of anxiety in this simple way.

It wasn't until seeing my most recent therapist, after the birth of my daughter, that this new concept finally clicked. She encouraged me, when I was describing a feeling of panic, to break it down further. To something more basic. She didn't want me to default to describe it as feeling anxious or having anxiety. Where I ended up, after sitting with that idea, was fear. For all I know, every other therapist I've ever worked with may have suggested something similar in different words, and maybe I just needed to hear it 9,000 times before I truly got it. But there was something that felt earth-moving about breaking open anxiety as fear.

Anxiety as fear seems far more relatable. When broken down into such a primal emotion, it actually loses some of its power for me. It seems less huge—less looming. It becomes normal and expected. Learning to lean into our fear requires lots of tools. For real. These tools will look different for everyone. For me, they include alone time, outdoor time, meditation in some capacity, playfulness, and connecting with family and friends. An active prescription for as-needed Ativan is also in my arsenal. This might not be a first-line tool for me, but it's an available tool nonetheless.

When handling the anxiety flavor of fear, we need to have lots of tools at the ready, and definitely not ones that are rusted-out and questionable.

(I'll note that not all anxiety is clinical in nature. Most of us experience it to some degree, and it doesn't always get in the way of our functioning in the day to day. But it can definitely hold us back from what could be possible.)

These tools can look like:

- Working with a therapist and/or psychiatrist,
- Working with a coach,
- Making mindset shifts,
- Making nutrition shifts,
- Exercising,
- Spending in nature,
- Meditating,
- Taking medications,
- Getting acupuncture,
- Receiving massage, and
- Seeing a chiropractor.

No one reading this should feel the least bit of shame if they rely on medication to help manage what we're covering here. I use it as one of my tools, and while it's only one tool and it's important to get loads more tools, it can help in certain situations and it's important to know that. Each of us does what we need.

The Differences between Therapy and Coaching

Since we're talking about tools, it seems like a good place to spend some time on a common area of curiosity: How are therapy and coaching different?

While the two services share some tools and roots in common, they are distinctly different offerings. A licensed clinical social worker who now offers coaching, I'm in a unique position to describe some of the main differences between the two. Try thinking of it this way:

Your Baseline/Day-to-Day Life
You're in a boat. You're riding the waves, sailing along. Sure, sometimes the water gets a bit choppy, but you're well-enough equipped to handle

all that the elements have to throw your way. You've got supplies, you've got resources, and you're good to go. Even when you get a bit thrown, you regain your footing and get back on your route.

Therapy
The waves have thrown you out of the boat. You're trying to stay afloat, and you can't quite get back into the boat on your own. You're trying, but you need some new skills and resources, and some additional support, to get back in. Or, you have some historic content you want to dive into. In other words, you want to go scuba diving. You're going to need an expert and proper gear to go there, but you're ready to dive into some exploration, discovery, and healing of the past. There is actual mental health diagnosis and *treatment* happening here.

Coaching
Here's what a person considering coaching might say: "This boat is great and all, but I'd like a different view. I'm ready to go parasailing. I want to see things from a different perspective and reach new heights. But, um, where do I start? What kind of equipment do I need?" Your coach is your parasailing partner. They are going to help you *sail in the sky*. They help you clarify your goals, learn new skills, and chart your course. There are all different kinds of coaches, from business coaches to health and wellness coaches. All of them can help you reach new heights.

***

This is clearly an oversimplification of these concepts, but it's a helpful way to start to understand. Many therapists are wonderful at using coaching-style techniques, and they can absolutely be implemented with certain clients. It's important to note, though, that it's a different service with different goals. Ethically, once you have provided therapy to a client (if you're a therapist), if they become interested in coaching, you would refer them to a different coach rather than coach them yourself. On the flip side, if one of your coaching clients needs therapy services, it is time to refer them out and not resume coaching work until they are ready/able.

Exercise Idea

Think about what tools you currently have on board for helping with fear. Do you see anxiety showing up in your life? What might happen if you shift to viewing it as a branch extending from fear?

CHAPTER 4
SLOW DOWN

Sometimes, fear can feel immobilizing. Other times, the *last* thing it wants is for us to sit still. It wants us to do *all the things*. It wants us to go, go, go!

When I'm in those times, it can feel hard to pace myself. I feel like I need to absorb all the information from a new book, blossom my article idea into a full-blown piece right at that moment, and more—almost as if my idea will escape, or I have to get it out before anyone else does—like once it found me it's more likely to find someone else too. It reminds me of how Elizabeth Gilbert describes ideas in *Big Magic*: as beings separate from us that are hoping to be born into reality. So, an idea keeps tapping you on the shoulder, essentially hoping you will sign on to work with it. If you keep putting it to the side, it will likely leave and find someone else to work with. Basically, ideas are free agents and can choose their best path to being created.

At the very core of my need for speed is fear. Fear that someone else will get that same idea out to the public before I do. Taking it a step further, it's fear that they will do it better. What happens when I get caught up in the whirlwind of wanting to make sure I'm first, is that I feel scattered, spent, and frantic. I lose sight of why I wanted to cultivate the idea in the first place! That doesn't feel good, and it's not what I want for myself or my life. And so "slow down" became a helpful mantra of mine.

When I was writing my first book, *Birth Story Brave*, the Universe was sending me all the signs to just take my time and slow down. The signs came by way of snails. Some were still alive; some had left their empty shells behind. While walking along the beach, I would find handfuls upon handfuls of empty, sand-smoothed snail shells. Working in the garden, a snail would carefully cross a giant vegetable leaf. One even greeted me on my porch one afternoon. It took longer than it probably should have (a note about the word *should*: It's a great indicator that there's some personal judgment going on. Here, notice that my fear of not being quick enough is showing up.) for me to realize that the world around me was trying to tell me something, but when I finally caught on, I leaned wholeheartedly into the idea that each time I found a snail it was a message just for me.

Go inward. Slow down.

Rather than listening to the voice of fear whispering the what-ifs, *slow down* reminds me that not everything needs to happen right at this moment and that there is an abundance of space in which to work on my idea. Sometimes I need to do some extra grounding exercises, or some meditation like yoga nidra to help me feel that calm, slow feeling. Being slow does not mean stopping. Being slow doesn't mean being unproductive. It means being intentional, mindful, inspired, and trusting.

We've talked about that immobilizing flavor of fear. Let's talk about the flip side of slowing down—not the flip side, really, but another layer. When fear has you in a corner, with you chewing off your fingernails like a cartoon character, you might *also* need to slow down, but in a different way. Rather than our body and physical energy needing to slow down, our mind and thought energy could benefit from taking the foot of the gas. Oftentimes, when we are feeling so paralyzed and haven't taken action around something in our lives, we can turn to our thoughts. Those thoughts might be having the best relay races ever, but they don't get to run (ha, see what I did there?) the show. This is where you step in and say, "Oh hey, fear. Slow down there. You are all over the place, but I'm going to go ahead and remind you that you don't drive. I do. I've got this."

Once you remind fear of its place, you can move forward with your plans. One. Step. At. A. Time. Sometimes our thoughts trick us into believing that the speedier and more robust our thought process, the more productive we're being. Total BS. But so many of us (me included) have bought into that idea more than once.

It's okay to be intentional about which thoughts you allow to take center stage and which you make a priority. The only real way to get things done (and done well) is to decide which are most meaningful to us, and then turn down the noise on all the other stuff fear creates in our minds.

Usually, when it comes to fear, we have at least a bit of choice. It might not feel like it when we're in the thick of it, but we do. We can stay stuck in fear, or we can move and shake a bit to get back to the life that lights us up. It's not often comfortable, and that's exactly the point. If we want to stay comfortable, we'll keep doing the same things that make us feel crazy over and over again. But wait—that doesn't sound so comfortable either, does it? So that's the choice: be uncomfortable by staying with the familiar or be uncomfortable by getting the heck out the situation that's driving you nuts. Be different. Be bold. Make progress. Go up.

Exercise Idea

Try yoga nidra. Yoga nidra means yogic sleep, and it is an absolutely delicious practice much like some other guided meditations, though it has some characteristics unique to itself. It is said to be restorative and restful. During our eight-week Mindfulness-Based Stress Reduction (MBSR) course, my husband and I got the chance to do in-person yoga nidra with the amazing Gina Sager multiple times. I have included her website, along with some others, in the Resources. Among yoga nidra recordings there are a whole range of recording lengths, imagery, and voices, so try lengths and recordings until you find one that works for you.

CHAPTER 5
REIKI

I still vividly remember the fear that I felt during my first Reiki attunement. Reiki is a relatively new (meaning within the last 100 or so years) energy healing technique with roots in Japan. It is gentle and promotes relaxation and stress reduction. Those attuned to Reiki are able to channel this healing energy, but they themselves do not create it. In other words, the energy does not come *from* them, but rather *through* them. There are multiple levels of training one receives prior to being able to teach and attune others, though you can practice on others even after you have completed Reiki I. (After Reiki II, you can start practicing on others professionally.)

As a Reiki master practitioner, I have completed three attunements, but the first one really left a huge impression. During my first attunement, I was pregnant with my daughter, my second child. During the meditation portion of the day, I sat on a chair, feet touching the floor. I expected to feel relaxed, but bit by bit I began to feel unbearably hot and somewhat lightheaded. Fear tapped on my shoulder.

Hey. Hey, what's going on? I bet something is wrong with your body. You're pregnant. You never know what could be happening in there.

I kept breathing, trying, hoping for my breath to anchor me and turn down the heat.

Seriously. You're about to pass out. I bet something is wrong with your heart. And whoa—won't you be embarrassed when you pass out in front of all these people? You're going to look so silly.

Eventually, I decided I definitely needed a backup to help me address the fear voice, which had convinced me I was about to fall out of my chair onto the floor. I stood up, shakily walked over to my Reiki teacher, and told her I felt like I was about to pass out. Luckily, she stayed super calm, and essentially told me to hang with it and that this was very likely part of my experience. She followed me back to my seat and placed her hands on my feet, giving me the grounding energy I so desperately needed to bring me back down. In my subsequent attunements, I specifically set the intention for the attunement to be gentle.

The point of this story is that, even in this deeply spiritual experience—or maybe *especially* in this deeply spiritual experience—fear wanted a front-row seat. It wasn't interested in standing by while I worked on shedding and letting go; it felt threatened. It wanted to point out the danger and have me hesitate. And I pushed through. I needed help to push through, but I still showed up. I was there and I hung with it. I came out of that attunement and meditation feeling powerful AF.

Even if you have gone through multiple layers of self-improvement or spiritual growth, fear can still pop in. It's okay. You're human. The presence of fear doesn't have to hold you back from advancing and growing. In fact, sometimes fear is the most likely to come in when we are taking big steps or pushing the limits of what has been familiar to us. It makes good sense to start to expect that fear will show up during these big transitions. Why wouldn't it make an appearance? Fear, since it wants to keep us safe, is going to put up all sorts of detour and danger signs to try to direct us back toward doing what we've always done. We don't have to go that route. Break out your map and chart a new course *despite* the roadblocks. And here's the thing: don't hesitate to ask for help to get to where you need to go. Stop at that gas station and ask for directions. Know that there are people around you who have gone before you and been where you've been. It doesn't make you any less strong to ask for assistance along your path.

CHAPTER 6
HEALTH SCARES

Have you ever had something come up with your health and totally overreacted to it? Or overanalyzed it until you thought you might be losing it?

One Friday afternoon, I got a phone call from my endocrinologist's office, letting me know that my recent blood work showed an elevated TSH (thyroid-stimulating hormone) level. They recommended an increase in my thyroid medication and a follow-up office visit. No big deal, right? Fast-forward to Saturday night, and I was in bed becoming increasingly sure that I could be dying.

Around 2012, I was diagnosed with Hashimoto's disease, an autoimmune disorder that impacts the whole body but is most commonly known for its impact on the thyroid gland. Luckily, I didn't develop hypothyroidism until 2015, after the birth of my son. Apparently pregnancy can make autoimmune disorders worse. High TSH can be accompanied by some uncomfortable side effects like fatigue, sensitivity to cold, and muscle aches. Irritability, anxiety, and heart palpitations are sprinkled in for me as well.

Was I actually in danger on that Saturday night? No. But my fear thoughts were having a full-on slumber party with pillow fights and late-night snacks.

What if there is actually something wrong with my heart?
Should I wake my husband?
What does this all mean? Why did my TSH go up in the first place?

Bottom line: Getting all worked up and freaked out over what *could* be going on with my body was not changing the outcome of what *was* going on. Except that stress is no good for autoimmune stuff. It was important to come back to the basics. Slow down. Trust. Know that things will work out as they have before.

Sparks

Some people, like me, are so very tuned-in to physical sensations in their body. This, as they will tell you, is often both a blessing and a curse. It's so helpful to know what's going on inside, or at least some idea of what might be happening, but therein lies the problem— when you don't know for sure, sometimes fear likes to make an appearance. And really, that just muddies the waters.

But guess what? This is exactly like so many times when fear makes an appearance. You get to remind it, "I've got this."

Exercise Idea

On a sheet of paper, draw an outline of a body. Using a pen or colored pencils, highlight the areas of sensations that feel uncomfortable in your physical body. On a scale from 1 to 10, with 10 being the most fear, note how much fear is associated with that feeling in your body. Imagine yourself sending love to all of these parts of your body, showing compassion and caring. You can even say to yourself, "You are loved. You are supported. You are safe."

CHAPTER 7
HOLDING BACK: WHAT'S POOP GOT TO DO WITH IT?

Ever have a time when you desperately need to go number two and public restrooms are the only option? Hesitantly, you scan the stalls when you walk in.

Damn it. There is a pair of feet under one of the stall doors.

You open a stall door and sit. You wait, and the poop standoff begins. So self-conscious are you about being judged based on your body's sounds or smells, you hold back like never before. Do you remember the flavor of fear called fear of embarrassment (from Chapter 1)? Or of what others think? The poop standoff embodies both of those *big time*.

Eventually, one of you will likely give up (or actually finish, who knows), maybe even giving a little performative flush and hand wash to trick the other person into thinking you actually did something other than sit and stare at the back of the metal stall door, planning and strategizing. If you *truly* need to let loose and waiting isn't an option, perhaps you wait until the other person flushes and then try to hurry and poop *all* the poop before the flush ends. (Speed pooping: not for the faint of heart.)

Hang with me here. Women especially seem to fall prey to what I've dubbed "the poop standoff." What is it? Essentially, it's another manifestation of fear. It's a way we hold ourselves back when we could be letting loose and being ourselves. And this is one a lot of us can relate to.

My husband stares open-mouthed at me as I describe the poop standoff concept to him. Apparently, this isn't a thing for guys. (Admittedly, he believes it's not a thing for anyone else and that I must be the only one imagining myself having a silent battle of the wills within those cold tile walls.)

My public bathroom behavior is ironic, as I hardly ever have the privilege of being in the bathroom without others in the room because of my kids. You might expect that feeling awkward about going to the bathroom in public wouldn't even occur to me. Yet, I've felt this way for as long as I can remember. Socialization, cultural cues, family—whatever it was, was. It really got me thinking about what a great metaphor this is. If at least some of us are holding back in front of *other humans* in the freaking bathroom of all places, *despite knowing that everyone poops*, in what other ways are we holding back?

The reasons for the poop standoff are grounded in fear of being judged/being seen as gross/being humiliated/being offensive. Where else do these fears and insecurities pop up in our lives? Goodness, the list could be endless. The point is, though, that if we are holding back in the most basic of ways, could it be likely that we are holding back in other areas? And if we don't want fear to drive in our lives, do we really want it to sit next to us when we're on the toilet?

I fully embraced this whole freedom idea while shopping in a department store recently. Sitting there, on that hard seat, I realized I was doing no one any favors by holding back. I don't coach people to suppress their needs and hide. I help them to feel authentic and put their needs front and center! That is a true releasing of fear (and whatever else).

CHAPTER 8
HOW FEAR PROTECTS US

It can be all too easy to be swept up in the idea that fear is something to be resisted and shut out. Some people in your life might even suggest that ignoring fear or pretending it isn't there is the way to handle its role in your life. Ignoring fear covers up this important and essential truth about fear: It exists to protect us.

Fear plays the role of the person in the watchtower. Fear announces the arrival of possible threats, getting troops at the ready to neutralize whatever the threat at hand is. Does fear overreact and get the call wrong sometimes? You bet. That's why it's not the only one in the command center. You are there too, with the ability to hear the message and take space to sort out whether (or not) the alarm is warranted. I am absolutely getting a visual right now similar to the command center in the movie *Inside Out*. It seems, though, that unlike the film, there is an additional presence other than just the different emotions and feelings running amok and doing what they do best. There is also the overseer of the command center. That's you.

Many of us are absolutely unaware of the overseer, believing wholeheartedly that those alarms going off are the truth and what we need to pay attention to. It takes practice and commitment to pull back from those alarms again and again in order to see the big picture.

Is it possible to honor the role fear plays in our lives and not let it take over? I absolutely think so. We can have space for both compassion and boundaries in our lives (that doesn't apply only to fear)! We are served well by setting some boundaries with our emotions, in this case with fear.

Sparks

Exercise Idea

Who's in your command center? Which voice is the loudest? Which voice is the softest? As the overseer, where do you sit, and what does your space look like? Jot down your answers and make a sketch if you like. Which emotions or feelings do you need to work on setting firm boundaries with?

CHAPTER 9
DO THE WORK; DO IT ANYWAY

As I have leaned more and more into my business Instagram accounts, #dothework and #doitanyway have been two of my favorite hashtags to use. I also love #dowhatscaresyou. Even the simple act of using these reminds me why I do the work I do. Leveling up in my authenticity is something that is a delicious side effect of helping others find theirs. And doing it all in spite of what-ifs is that much more powerful.

Once you put the what-ifs in their place, a whole new world opens up. If you set them aside once, it becomes easier to do it again and again. Almost addictive, even. To be clear, there is not a reckless abandon for reason or safety. However, there is absolutely a curiosity. Am I not doing this thing because it scares me? Or are there solid, justifiable reasons for waiting or not acting?

There will be times when fear will trick you into thinking you have a justifiable reason for not taking action. If you suspect that might be what's happening in a given moment, go back to your gut feeling and knowing (which we will discuss more in Part Three) and check in with yourself. What matters most to you in this life? What are the things that excite you and make you feel inspired? If your action is aligned with those, the reason you're holding back is probably fear-based.

Once you know that fear is what's keeping you from moving forward, you get to work to release it. Determine the flavor of fear from Chapter 1. What story is it pointing toward? Stories are the repetitive belief systems that frame how we view ourselves and the world. They usually start when we are quite young, and often are generated from an adult in our lives. Over time, we look for evidence to support the stories, and you don't usually notice the fact that the story might not be true or accurate at all. If you have a story of "I am unlovable," maybe your fear is highlighting that by holding you back from finding a partner. You isolate yourself, look down, avoid engaging with strangers. What if you shift the story so fear has nothing to highlight? "I am unlovable" can become "I am worthy and ready to connect." You decide. Release what is no longer serving you.

CHAPTER 10
FILTER OUT THE FEAR-BASED CRUD

When I first started offering coaching, I remember devouring a workbook on building coaching skills until I realized the author was using some of the fear-based motivators that I was working to erase from my life. The author said something to the effect of "If you want your practice to succeed, you will do this. Otherwise, you clearly don't care much about your practice and it will fail." Major turnoff. Obviously I didn't want my practice to fail. But I also didn't want someone to scare me into doing things their way. I sure as hell didn't become an entrepreneur to be forced to do things someone else's way. What that guy wrote immediately made me not want to give him any more of my money.

This is just one example of the fear-based crud that we take in on a daily basis. Once you tune in to how much people play into these messages, you will start to see them *everywhere*. At first, I think it's a bit alarming. But here's the great thing: Once you're aware, you get to choose, to an extent, what you take in and what you filter out.

Here's an example: Most times when we hop on the Internet—to check e-mail, to buy something, to listen to music—we're hit with a ton of messages. Many are marketing to us, hoping for a click, while some are news-based. *Buy this armored cover to protect your grill from predators! Watch tonight to learn about the dangers of loving your partner.* My husband and I still joke about a radio ad we heard years ago that said, "There's nothing worse than a dead battery." We can think of some things.

Here's something that some ads and some news articles have in common: They play on fear to get us to pay attention and act. That's not okay with me. Give me the facts, but don't try to freak me out, okay? It's one thing if the content of the news is heavy or sad or informative (we have some responsibility to see what is going on in the world, even if it is hard to bear witness to), but it's another if things are twisted and shaped especially to grab you. Ick.

Once you start to see the places where fear pops up externally (Don't we already have enough internal battles with fear? We don't need the external stuff too.), you can start to make choices about what you take in and what you let slide to the side. That might look like unfollowing someone on Instagram who posts messages about things you *need* to do. That might look like changing your Internet home page to a different news network (or not news). And, it could even look like unfollowing some friends on Facebook if they are spewing fear-based crud. That part is up to you.

CHAPTER 11
WHAT THEY THINK IS . . .
WHAT THEY THINK

In October 2017, I launched the digital version of my first-ever book, *Birth Story Brave*. It didn't change the world and it wasn't an overnight success, but it changed everything about what I thought was possible for me. As soon as I launched the print version of *Birth Story Brave* a month later, I backpedaled on the word *book*.

My inner critic argued, "It's too thin. You can't call this a book! It's not like it's a novel. Ha! People will be disappointed that they spent money on this!" During more than one podcast interview, I refused to call it a book. "It's a guide!" I insisted. My fear of what others think was showing.

At not quite 50 pages, *Birth Story Brave* is and was exactly what it was always meant to be: an accessible way for moms to reflect on their childbirth experiences without being weighed down by lots of reading. It was more about them creating their content than me sharing mine.

What I didn't realize at first was that by changing the classification of my book during conversation (it is a guide, but . . . can't it be both?), I was doing two things: I was cheapening the value and impact of my own work, and I was falling into the trap of what Dr. Michael Gervais describes as the greatest fear in today's world. It's one of my favorite quotes, and even though I shared it once before, here it is again for emphasis: "The greatest fear in modern times is what other people think. . . . Our job is to love others and not give a shit what they think of us."

What I know to be true, and what I have always believed, is that *Birth Story Brave* is a meaningful, unique tool that the world needs. What I grew to discover and lean into is that it *is* a book, and that I don't need to hide by trying to switch around words just because someone (or many people) could judge me and say that I shouldn't dare call it a book. As I walk the path with those tuning into their true identities, I have learned this lesson in my training: My work is powerful, my work is valuable, and my work is part of my growth.

What other people think is exactly that: It's what they think. It's not the truth or anything close to it. It is their assessment of how things are through their lens. What people think is filtered through their own stories and ideas and beliefs—and, well, we know how messy that can get. My point is this: You get some say in determining your truth. Please, please do not base it on what other people think.

CHAPTER 12
WHAT'S UNDER THE FEAR?

As we've touched on a bit already, there is usually something hanging out under our fear (a thought, a memory, a belief). If we can be brave enough to dig into that, there usually is an opportunity for growth. (My husband and I always tell our kids that being brave is being scared and doing something anyway.) It's almost as though you're pulling away thick, overgrown, invasive vines to reveal a beautiful, solid oak tree underneath. But before you get to that solid tree, there is a layer of spiderwebs (beliefs/thoughts) to familiarize yourself with. And what do many of us do when we touch spiderwebs? Recoil. Because bites or poison, or just ick. We have to get through the ick to get to the beautiful, solid foundation.

So, what kinds of things are under there, making up the spiderwebs? *Old* stuff. Really stinking old stuff. Usually, these are beliefs or stories you made up about yourself when you were a wee one. We all do this. Something happens or we experience something our parents do or say, and we make it mean something about who we are as a person. It doesn't stop there. Then we gather evidence upon evidence to support that story, even if there are lots of other glorious stories we could be telling ourselves. At that point we have blinders on, though. We don't see the other stories until the library gets new lighting. These are stories such as:

- I am stupid.
- I am unworthy.
- I am unlovable.
- I am ugly.
- I am weak.

The really incredible thing is that we usually don't see that we have these stories until someone points them out or we uncover them. They're invisible to us. Until we do some archaeology about what's driving our current thoughts and behaviors, they have a way of staying very well hidden. The great news is they don't need to stay hidden, and once we become aware of them, it can become easier and easier to spot when we're in the middle of collecting evidence to support a false story.

We can even rewrite our stories and set intentions to flip them. "I am weak" becomes "I am strong" or "I feel fear and am still strong." "I am unlovable" becomes "I am unique and appealing just as I am." The key is to not allow our stories to continue to define us. Close that book and start a new one. Allow the old story to expire and pick a fresh one from the shelf. It's waiting for you.

Exercise Idea
What are your biggest, loudest stories? Write down the first few that come to mind. Practice rewriting them to flip them into more empowering versions.

CHAPTER 13
SETTING THE INTENTION TO RELEASE FEAR

2018 was a year of shedding and releasing for me. I dug into expectations, emotions, and beliefs, and let them go. Some of them were more stubborn than others, and I might keep saying *hi* to those for a bit. Fear was one of the most deeply held things of all. It was *in* me. It's in all of us. But I was really listening to it, with the volume turned up—to more than a "this is a good song" volume. This was not a fear-for-my-life kind of fear, but the kind of just being afraid to show up in the world as I am, without caring what people think. I wanted to be done with it controlling my actions and with listening to the what-ifs it whispered in my ear.

This fear of mine felt so old. I would take steps forward, and then feel stuck again. When I was ready for the next level of help with moving this transition along, I scheduled a session with my Reiki master/teacher, Mary. She completed two out of my three attunements, and she's this vibrant, loving, interesting woman. Her living room, where we had our Reiki trainings, is the kind where you could just hang out in for the whole day. Cozy and clean—but not so clean that you're scared to touch things. Her whole house has this vibe of acceptance and spiritual advancement. You just want to soak it all up. At the beginning of a Reiki session, you set an intention for what you would like to accomplish. I absolutely, without a doubt, wanted to let go of whatever fear was holding me back from my next steps. During our hour-long session, Mary held a beautiful space for me as she channeled Reiki energy and led me through a powerful visualization that changed how I felt about the fear I had been holding onto. I said hello to a past lifetime during which I was controlled by my fear of persecution. I felt that I was actually able to enter into this past life and take away the fear I had experienced long ago. By doing this, I could feel

Sparks

I would be freed to experience and develop all sorts of new creativity. My fear was not entirely gone, but it was no longer stuck. It was moving, flowing, and changing. I will be entirely honest in saying that once things get moving again, it doesn't always feel great. In this instance, I felt an initial rush of relief, followed by some other times of challenges as things continued to process. And that was just one layer of fear! I wonder how many are stacked up, waiting to be explored.

Exercise Idea

When we are ready to move through fear, it can be helpful to set an intention to do so. An intention need not be complicated; it is a statement of what you hope to do. Write or say the statement in the present tense, like "I am releasing fear" or "I am letting my fear move." This statement helps keep you focused and reminds you what you're doing. It can also remind you that you have the strength to do the work, because it's not always easy.

PART TWO

AMUSEMENT

The word *amusement* might not be one that you think of often in terms of how you view life overall or your life specifically. You might think of an amusement park but then stop short there. What does it really mean to use it in your mindset—in how you think about things?

I've settled on lighthearted entertainment. It's the perspective of "Hmm, that's interesting." We can be entertained or fascinated not only by easy or happy things, but by challenging ones as well. Within amusement is the acceptance that things can be interesting despite their toughness, their power, or their beauty.

Some other words that come to mind when I think about amusement are *wonder* and *amazement*. Regarding an event or a thing with wonder—the big-eyed stare of a child, for example—can absolutely shift our way of being with the world.

I suppose life doesn't *have* to occur to you as interesting. It's certainly a choice to make. For me, if I could see the value in tuning into that amusement during meditation, I wondered what would happen if I could summon it outside of meditation as well. Bit by bit, I practiced tuning in more and more to the amazement of it all. This life. The things that it offers and the things that it takes. The hurt, the pain, the struggles, the love, the joy, the warmth. All of it. Interestingly, shifting your lens to view things—even the tough stuff—as amusing makes life feel quite a bit lighter.

Put together, my recipe for amusement looks something like this:

1. Lighthearted entertainment
2. Acceptance
3. Wonder
4. Amazement

Your recipe might look a bit different. You may find that you add a sprinkle more of this or a dash less of that. Or maybe you have a secret ingredient. The key to amusement is finding the unique blend of elements that make the corners of your mouth turn up ever so slightly, not necessarily in a smile but in a shift and an opening.

Lighthearted Entertainment

We've touched on this already, but just for clarity's sake, let's review. I see this as being in a state of being entertained by something in our lives from a place of openness. It's so difficult to avoid describing and defining these terms without using some of the other words, because they are so intertwined! In amusement, something can be entertaining without necessarily being pleasant. So, we can have difficult things happen to us while maintaining amazement and wonder.

In lightheartedness, we keep things from being too heavy. Ascribing meaning or over-analyzing can add weight to a situation or event, or even a brief or simple experience. For clarity's sake, know that I am a huge fan of self-reflection—but intentional self-reflection. By intentional, I mean taking time aside *on purpose* to think, not getting wrapped up in a whirlwind of analyses.

Per Merriam-Webster.com, lighthearted is defined as "free from care, anxiety, or seriousness." They also note "cheerfully optimistic and hopeful." There is an absence of worry. And did you notice how they mention anxiety? Think about how I connected anxiety and fear in Part One. If there is an absence of anxiety, fear likely does not have a place, either, which opens the door to amusement.

As I was going through the first round of edits for this book, I was beginning to read *The Brave Learner*, a book on homeschooling by Julie Bogart. I stopped in my (visual) tracks when I read her description of enchantment, a word she uses throughout her book, because it made me think of everything I'm talking about here. She says: "To me, an enchanted *life* is living in my ordinary circumstances with heightened awareness—being on the lookout for a 'surprise of happy.'" Absolute swoon. This woman gets me, and clearly her definition goes right in line with lighthearted entertainment and amusement.

Acceptance

Regarding life with amusement or lighthearted entertainment has an undercurrent of another powerful way of seeing life and what happens in it: acceptance. Getting to a place of regarding things—even tough things—from a place of amusement, has a prerequisite of accepting that this is the way things are, at least in this moment. Once you get to the place of acceptance, it's not actually that far of a leap to amusement.

This sucks and I don't want it. → This sucks, but it is what's happening and I can sit with it. → This sucks and, wow, I never realized how rocked I get by feeling discomfort. I can even feel it in my stomach! (Note the awareness!)

By accepting things as they are, we remove resistance to whatever it is we are dealing with at hand. We no longer wish things outside of our control were different than they are. Pushing against what *is* creates conflict within us, making it more difficult to get to a place of wonder or entertainment, not to mention happiness or joy. For instance, if my car gets hit and there is a huge dent on the side, I can choose to focus on how unfair that is and wonder why it happened to me, or I can know those focuses don't change the fact that it happened and definitely won't get my car repaired. Rather, I can accept the dent and decide which steps I would like to take next (attempting to contact the person who hit it, calling my insurance company, etc.).

Fear encourages us to resist the way things are because it would prefer that we dig in and live in the past or future rather than sitting with the potential discomfort of the present. If we stay wrapped up in our stories of something being unfair or challenging, we don't get to break free to see what is *really* underneath.

A note on acceptance: I do not mean—and do not mistake that I am suggesting—that we let injustices persist and/or abuses continue. Acceptance gives us a starting point of relating to things outside of our control, however, of *this is how things are* and *this is where we are going to go from here*. It allows us to acknowledge things as they are without resisting them due to fear or hiding behind the creation of an alternate reality.

Wonder and Amazement

I'm going to wrap these two friends together because they are so closely related. Think of a time that you stopped in your tracks because of the beauty of something, or the size of something, or the unbelievability of something. The kind of thing that leaves your mouth hanging wide open, and your eyes huge. Now, scale it back a touch.

There is no doubt that the word *amazing* is a bit overused in our society. You might think, *That chicken salad sandwich you had for lunch was* amazing? *Really?* I get it. It seems a bit silly or even impossible to feel amazed by so many things day in and day out. And yet, what if we were? What if we held the perspective of and saw life through the lens of being amazed that we are in this body, in this lifetime, having this experience? What if there was a tiny bit of open-mouthed wonder or even just a slight-mouth-gap wonder at even the most mundane things that we experience?

Experiencing life from that place sounds so much more enjoyable to me. In that place maybe you can appreciate, on a whole new level, the way chicken, mayo, celery, cranberries, and almonds are joined in deliciousness. The people upset with how you choose to describe your lunch are most definitely inside their own stories about life's qualities. You don't have to match their story.

Shifting your mindset takes work and practice. You likely will not (and if you do, wow!) find amusement in everything that happens to you. What you can do is practice seeing how it comes up for you and run mini experiments to see how shifting your mindset changes your experience of this life. When you find yourself looking around grumpily, or frowning, take a moment to just tune into your senses. What are you hearing? Raindrops? Birds? Maybe put on a song that makes you feel good. And what do you see? Is there anything funny around you? Anything beautiful? Practice looking for and being open to these sorts of fun surprises.

CHAPTER 14
LIGHTING YOUR FIRE

So once you're through with allowing fear to snuff out your inner flame, what do you do? How do you feed that spark? Part of the magic is that in journeying through fear, the act alone seems to ignite your fire. It takes courage and trust, and when you see those qualities in yourself, it seems to light up an inner desire.

When I was working as a therapist in a group practice setting, I worked mostly with clients navigating anxiety and depression. When they would confront fear and move through it, you could see a transformation—not just in their faces and eyes (because there's that twinkle), but also in their overall energy and actions. Doing the things that scared them actually changed what they believed was possible, as if a veil had been lifted. I had a client who would track his progress and a-ha moments in a little notebook or on a scrap piece of paper every week, and I always looked forward to hearing about his new-found insights. It's so inspiring to see people doing the hard work and reaping the benefits.

I once had a therapist (my own, that is) tell me that activity begets activity, and though as I recall he was talking about sexual activity (don't worry: totally relevant when you're taking an antidepressant and sex drive is *low*) it seems this is the case with many actions we choose to take. Once we get the ball rolling, it creates momentum and thus space for all sorts of growth to occur.

Amusement is absolutely no different. Once you find a bit here, and then notice it there, and *Hey, there it is over there*, before you know it, you hardly have to think about creating the shift anymore. It's just there. Clearly some of us will need to work at this more than others; some humans seem more inclined toward amusement than others. Just like any skill that we acquire and cultivate, there will be times that feel like setbacks. That's part of it. It's part of growth that's to be expected.

Exercise Idea

Carol Dweck, a psychology professor and researcher, explains with great clarity the concept of not quite being good at something yet and expecting it as part of the learning process. She has done extensive research on learning and embraces the notion of having a "growth mindset," which allows for the learner to be imperfect at something and gain more mastery with practice. She compares this to a "fixed mindset," which is the idea that we either have a skill or we don't, and we don't subscribe to the idea that we can gain mastery the more we try something. Watch one of Carol Dweck's videos explaining this. You can Google "Carol Dweck and growth mindset." (I've also included one of my favorite videos in the Resources section.)

What do you feel you've practiced in your own life? When it comes to amusement, a growth mindset is key. You can get better at experiencing it and noticing it the more you practice!

CHAPTER 15
MEETING AMUSEMENT

When my daughter was not quite 1 year old, I decided that I wanted to take my spiritual life to the next step by enrolling in a year-long intuitive training and self-healing program. One year. Fifty-two weeks. That's a long haul, and while it felt like such a long period of time at the beginning of the course, it ended up going by in the blink of an eye. I wanted to deepen my spiritual practice and really lean into that voice that kept whispering, *Um, so, you're really meant to do this kind of work, and I've been trying to be patient, but now it's time.*

The distance version of the program, which I happily participated in (I'm in Maryland and my teacher, Stacia Synnestvedt, is in Colorado), has weekly meditations at its core, during which you learn tools and techniques for reading and healing your own energy, as well as for reading others' energy. Setting energetic boundaries is another large part of the coursework. Empaths in particular have difficulty with absorbing energy from those around them and can end up experiencing feels that aren't even their own!

The visualizations that Stacia uses are vibrant and purposeful. One of the things that she refers to often is setting the intention to view things we perceive during meditation from a place of *amusement*. And I swear, even that word on its own brings, at the very least, a half-smile to my lips. Once you see things from a place of amusement, your whole perspective shifts.

I will talk more about my journey with intuition and knowing later in Part Two, but having the introduction to amusement in this context felt like coming home. It felt like a description of what my true nature of relating to life is. The me who would show through in glimpses throughout my childhood. The silly me, the carefree me, albeit the one who was often

Sparks

told to calm down and not laugh so loudly. The one not swallowed up by anxiety. And wow, was it good to see that me.

CHAPTER 16
SHARE YOUR FEARS, INCREASE AMUSEMENT AND TRUST

> "The only way to ease our fear and be truly happy is to acknowledge our fear and look deeply at its source."
> ~ Thich Nhat Hanh in *Fear*

Have you ever had one of those neurotic AF moments? They can cause us to spiral if we're not aware of what's happening (and yep, that happens sometimes). Sharing about them with someone close to us can help to ground us and bring us back to reality, calling out the fear for what it is. Then you might even be able to get to the place of "Whoa, how interesting that my mind took me on this ride" (more on that later in the book).

Here's one of my neurotic moments from today: Someone I follow on Instagram has a similar feel to her business and offerings—not identical, just similar. With my coaching packages, I offer Reiki as an option. That way, when clients decide they would like to have some energy work as part of a session or for an entire session, that's already an option built into our agreement. The other person offers coaching, but instead of Reiki, she offers Tarot card readings. Apparently this activates my fear on some level, because my mind's first reaction was to interpret the existence of her business as competition. It really got my voices of "She's probably doing it better" and "There aren't enough clients for both of us!" going. Do you hear the fear of scarcity there?

Back to the Instagram Story. All it took for my fear to have a great old time was to see an Instagram Story this woman posted that said, "Have you found your spark?" Oh man. I saw the word *spark* and immediately thought, *Wait! No! That word is in my book title! She's going to think I stole it from her—but it's my nickname! And I'm already writing it! What if someone else is going to publish my book idea before I do?*

Slow down, Emily. Luckily, it didn't take long to get real with myself. I realized a couple of things:

1. Her post immediately before the spark one was about a hummingbird, which is a powerful spiritual symbol for me right now. It's one that came up in the Reiki session I mentioned at the end of Part One.
2. Another way I could have received her post, especially as it came right after the bird, was validation that I'm on the right track with my work.

How funny! My mind went right to fear, but I didn't let myself get too caught up in it this particular time. I caught it. Catching yourself in the act takes practice, and believe me when I say that I don't always do it! What's more, I shared with my husband my initial reaction and thought process, which further highlighted how irrational it really was. He gave me a reality check. When we share our mental processes with others, we might find out that we're not all that alone in them, and it can help us find some humor in how our thoughts manifest. It changes both how we relate to and how we show up in the world. And that's big.

As a brief aside, when you surround yourself with people who are doing similar work to yours and who have similar mindsets and ideals, it is inspiring and feels so supportive. It's also a good idea to keep in mind that it absolutely skews your perception of how many of these people exist in the world and how many people are or are not familiar with the skills and knowledge that you (and this group of people you're in) know. In other words, it can be fuel to a fear of your skill set not being unique and needed. Let me pause here to highlight that it is fuel for an *irrational* fear. Should we stop following people who have similar business models and values? Absolutely not. But there is weight to remaining conscious of the lens that our surroundings cause us to have.

Exercise Idea

Who are your go-to people for a reality check? Make a list. Check in with at least one of them once this week to test whether your lens could benefit from some recalibration. Even better, set a reminder to check in with someone once each week.

CHAPTER 17
FINDING AMUSEMENT IN THE SPLATTER

As I write this, my daughter is in a season of throwing things. She's 22 months old, and as soon as she is done with something, she wants it out of her space so she can welcome into her space whatever it is she's ready for next. Out with the muffin to make room for the apple juice. Out with the dolls to make room for the cars. Out with the (lidless) cup of water to make room for . . . I don't know, air? When she's done, she's just done. As a side note, imagine if, when we were finished with something, we could release so easily. Emotions, too. Toddlers have a brilliant way of releasing anger to give way to joy. They feel what they feel when they feel it.

But back to the throwing. For breakfast the other day, I made strawberry-banana smoothies for my son and daughter. I poured the thick, pink liquid into two cups, put a stainless straw in each, and set them on the table in front of the two most adorable faces I see each day. (At this point, you're probably asking yourself why I haven't learned to put lids on more of my daughter's drinks. That's fair.) A few minutes went by, and I savored the peace in the kitchen as my littles drank their smoothies. And then: *splat*. I recognized that noise.

Pink liquid all over the floor (and on the dog's face—win for him!). I sucked in my breath, and then something I saw made me pause. I paused and actually *smiled*. In the center of the biggest splat on the floor was a very distinct pink heart. The thrown smoothie actually made a heart. How?

Amusement is (sometimes quite literally) finding the heart in the splatter. The love note in milk, frozen strawberries, banana, and peanut butter. If we don't pause, we don't see the note. When irritation and frustration blind us, which is only natural sometimes, the Universe sometimes tries to pass us a love note and we miss it. I want to see all the love notes that I can. Practicing amusement and living in lighthearted entertainment is the gateway for that. Amusement leaves us open to receiving and perceiving.

Exercise Idea

The next time you're frustrated, take a deep breath and pause. Turn up the corners of your mouth slightly and see what change that invites in. You might feel awkward as anything, because you're not used to doing that. But inviting in a smile, even a tiny fake one, sends your brain a different message. It interrupts the flow, in a good way. It throws out the irritation to make room for the _____. You get to fill in the blank.

CHAPTER 18
LIFE IS MESSY

I once heard someone say that toddler behavior feels less frustrating if you envision those little humans in tiny white lab coats. In other words, if you remember that they're doing what they're meant to do (experimenting), it's a lot easier to accept. I'm *pretty* sure it would make life a whole lot more amusing if we imagined *everyone* in white lab coats. Experimenting. Figuring this life out. Isn't that what we're all doing? And let's face it: Even if you don't have kids, life is messy.

We all have different histories, but each of us is in our current body for the first (and only) time ever. This lifetime. It's never happened before! Let this be our chance to experiment, through amusement, with this array of experiences before us.

I don't think I will ever forget a time-of-sickness story told to me by my friend Lily. It's not just the story itself; it was the *way* she told it. Now, to be fair, I think there was a bit of time between when the event happened and when she was recounting it, but there was a lightness and amusement to the story that was so refreshing to hear. It made the story so, well, entertaining. It was told through a different lens.

Lily's youngest had a stomach bug. (Why do those things always seem to crop up in the middle of the night?) The poor little guy needed to be rushed to the bathroom by Lily's husband. He barely made it to the tile floor before the bug made a visit. Lily's husband fell victim to the wet substance on the slippery floor and went down, taking the little guy as well. Both son and father were on the floor in vomit, dad having thrown out his back.

Clearly, on the night that this happened, this sucked. This is exactly the way you don't want to be awakened in the middle of the night. What struck me was that Lily found a place of amusement and relayed the story through that filter. As both a teller and a listener, it makes for a much different experience for a story to come from a place of amusement. It feels lighter, allows for more resilience, and can add to an arsenal of things we'll laugh about for a while, even if they weren't exactly funny when they happened.

Life can quite literally be messy (or downright filthy) sometimes, and that doesn't need to mean that it isn't amusing.

Exercise Idea

Rewrite one of your messy stories. Think about a time in the past when you had a truly messy experience. This doesn't have to be physically messy, just when you felt things were a mess or you were a mess. Retell the story looking for silver linings. What sort of unexpected things were uncovered?

CHAPTER 19
BARK IN MY TEETH

This morning, I took my son to preschool, just like I do two mornings every week. I walked him in, chatted with some of the other parents and his teachers (in true Emily, smile-filled style), and walked back to my car. As I sat back in the driver's seat, I flashed a grin at myself in the rearview mirror, which is something I often do. Teeth check, I guess?

Wait—what is that??

You see, prior to running out the door, I had grabbed a handful of raw almonds and a piece of dark chocolate, and deposited them immediately in my mouth to make a super-delicious combination of yum.

So what could that be nestled barely in between but more like *on top of* my teeth? A big piece of almond skin.

Oh hey there, friend. Tagging along for a ride?

I had talked to at least four different people, face-to-face, in my son's school. Not *one* person said anything about what looked to be a piece of tree bark hanging out in my mouth. This was no tiny piece of food that *maybe* they didn't see. It looked like perhaps I had brushed my teeth with a tree branch that morning.

At some points in my life, I would have been absolutely horrified. In my mind, I would have played over and over again my conversations with various people to try to remember their facial expressions. I would have felt so embarrassed. And I would have been nervous to see them the next time—and would probably make some ridiculous joke about it to them so they knew I *knew* they probably knew.

This morning, all I really did was smile. After the initial surprise of finding a sapling sprouting in my teeth, I quickly found amusement. It showed up like a supportive friend, offering a giggle rather than a gasp. If fear was there, it was definitely more of a whisper than a wail.

Sparks

The takeaways I offer for you are these:

1. Something that might be embarrassing to others (including your past self) does not necessarily have to be embarrassing to you. It can even be funny.
2. Even though fear tells you that people are hyper-aware of your appearance, they probably release any awareness as soon as your interaction ends. So maybe you can let it go too.
3. Give your teeth a little once-over after you eat nuts with skin.

CHAPTER 20
SING IT

I've gotten in the habit of doing little things that scare me regularly. It keeps my creativity alive and my belief in myself fueled. Ultimately, it builds the confidence I need to act despite feeling fearful. If I can do even tiny things on a regular basis, it makes the larger ones not feel so terrifying. One of my favorites is the time I sang on my Instagram Story. For me, this was a big deal. Singing was a gigantic part of my life as I was growing up. I loved humming and singing along to songs, learning lyrics and hearing my voice in my ears. I always participated in the school chorus, and for many years from middle school through high school, I was a member of the Johns Hopkins Peabody Children's Chorus, getting to sing at the Meyerhoff Symphony Hall in Baltimore and go on a tour in England and France.

I would only sing as part of a group or in front of people who knew me well. Despite my joy of singing, I shrank from solo opportunities, even though my instructors tried to encourage me. I was terrified. I didn't want to be seen!

At some point it occurred to me that it would be an excellent idea to sing on my Instagram Story and freaking *get over it*. Or at least start. My son and I had been rocking out almost daily to "High Hopes" by Panic! At The Disco, and it just felt right. No, I didn't sing the whole song (eek!), but a few lines.

I felt so powerful after that. Not because I wasn't scared or nervous, but because I *did it anyway!* I did exactly the thing we are always coaching our kiddos to do: try it even if you're not sure. Give it a chance even if you don't know if you'll like it. Do it even if you're scared. That's what it means to be brave. Singing on Instagram isn't changing any of society's challenges, but does the practice of change not start in small places? We can first experiment with putting ourselves out there in smaller ways before diving in with a cannonball.

Exercise Idea

What's one small thing you could do to put yourself out there today? Give a stranger a compliment? Reach out to someone you haven't talked to in a long time? Share a painting you did publicly? It doesn't need to be a 10 out of 10 on the scariness scale to be effective and give you a benefit. Choose something that feels like a 3 or 4, and go for it!

CHAPTER 21
DEEP JOY

> "Joy feels like happiness, only better. It's generated from within and doesn't depend on what we have or haven't got. It's vital for our well-being and arises in the moment. Joy connects us with a sense of the divine."
> ~ Gillian Anderson and Jennifer Nadel from *We: A Manifesto for Women Everywhere*

When I channel Reiki, and when I do therapy with or coach clients, I experience this deep joy that I can only categorize as amusement. It's as though the thing that lights me up the most has been ignited and tapped into, and at the very same time I'm in awe at the very feeling existing at all in the first place. The feeling doesn't just go away at the end of a session, either. It lasts! There is a wonder of getting to do this work, and it feeds me. The funny thing is, I don't know for sure that I was hungry for it until I started shifting my awareness to the present and to my experience.

I was hungry, don't get me wrong, but I didn't know what I could use to fill me up. I did what a lot of us do: I sort of buzzed around from thing to thing hoping that it would be the one to stick—and when it wasn't, I still felt empty and disillusioned. Guys? Nope. Lots of pot? Nope. All the exercise? Nope. Mindfulness? Holy crap, there's something there. The reason something was there was because I was there. I wasn't getting away from the root of it all, I was digging into it.

The thing that cultivates deep joy for one will certainly not be the thing that creates it for others. Knitting, writing, tightrope walking—your brand is going to be yours and yours alone. I have found throughout the years that the things that bring out the deep joy are often the most basic things: impromptu dance parties with my kids, hikes along trails through the woods, a conversation with a friend in the darkness of a summer evening, mug of tea or glass of wine in hand. The element of surprise is something that also adds to the joy, and this is where amusement comes in. When something catches us off guard, and we are primed to view it from a place of amusement, our entire experience changes.

Exercise Idea
What brings you deep joy? Make a list. When you're feeling off, pull out your list and choose something to do. Amusement loves spontaneity!

CHAPTER 22
SNUGGLES

Some days of motherhood leave me wondering whether I have a bit of mild depression. Especially in the long days of winter or in the middle of the summer, it creeps up on me when I start to feel held down or suppressed in my creativity. I turn irritable, sluggish, and frustrated. It's not long though before something blows through the smog and starts to light things up.

Remember that deep joy I just talked about? I also get that feeling when I'm snuggling with my kiddos in a big pile. When we're all a tangle of arms and legs and warmth, it's magic. All it takes is a lean of a little cheek on mine to start to thaw my iciness. I won't say that the heaviness doesn't come back at times (it does), but the ability to tune in to the pleasantness of the present moment anchors me. When I'm getting my hair pulled, that's a different story. That is me experiencing the *un*-pleasantness of the present moment. That's not nearly as easy for me to sit with, because it amplifies my feelings of frustration. But just the same, it pulls me (literally) into the present.

Let me make a note here for clarification. It is not my kids' responsibility to pull me out of low feelings or comfort me. As a parent, that's *my* job, not theirs. It just happens that one of the many things that is a powerful attention-grabber is the Souder Snuggle. (And a note to my husband: Sorry, hon. I didn't mean to leave you out of the snuggle dialogue. You are absolutely an integral part. ☺)

Finding the present moment is an absolute gift. It's not that the present is always pleasant, but it's what is actually happening. It's real. As my mindfulness teacher Gina Sager would say, "It's all we know we have for sure." We spend so much time in the past and the future, it can be a relief to realize that right here, right now, there are things happening that don't require much thought.

Exercise Idea

Do certain things in your life pull you more into the present moment than others? What do those things have in common? Do they involve the senses? Which ones? For example, snuggling with my kids activates touch, of course, but also smell. A parent does stop smelling their kids' hair one day, right?

CHAPTER 23
BONE BROTH AND ICE CREAM

Comfort and nurturing are pathways to opening. When we feel supported, we are more likely to want to open, or to be able to open. Comfort, as in the softness of flannel or the warmth of a cup of tea, holds us. Nurturing, through nourishment or spiritual practice, supports us in a different way.

One cold winter morning, both of my kiddos had the flu. The trees outside were coated in ice, some bending under the heavy weight. It had been a stressful couple of days, with sleepless nights and little arms clinging to me. To complicate things, our bull terrier, Cooper, had been sick with a stomach bug for the same period of time. He was at the vet, receiving fluids and anti-nausea medication.

I rarely have moments by myself in our kitchen. Even if the kids or my husband isn't there, the dog is usually curled up in his bed or looking up hopefully at me. On this day, the kitchen was quiet. My daughter was napping and my son was watching a show, taking it easy on his little body.

It was lunchtime. We had all sorts of things to eat, but I gravitated toward the things I want when I'm sick (even though I was perfectly healthy). I fixed a bowl of rice and homemade bone broth brought over by a friend. To be honest, this was my second bowl. I ate the first while my daughter fell asleep on my lap, her little eyelids getting heavier and heavier. I sat, thankful for the time by myself. It felt decadent, and some guilt started to creep in. I noticed it and moved through the uncomfortable feeling. Spoonful by spoonful, I emptied the bowl of broth and rice. It reminded me of the book I just read: *Kitchen Yarns* by Ann Hood, in which she talks about food as love. This moment felt like love.

After my bowl was empty, I found my way over to the freezer and put in a couple scoops of chocolate-peanut butter ice cream. Same bowl. No need for extra dishes, especially right then. It felt like a funny combination, to have ice cream after the simple broth and rice, but it worked. It was just what I needed. Rather than being a mindless cannonball into food as a distraction, this felt more like a warm hug.

My point in bringing this story into the mix is to highlight how seemingly conflicting things can exist side-by-side. Both can serve a purpose, and both are valuable. We don't have to push one out to welcome the other. They can both be welcome, but we get to call the shots on how much, what flavor, and so forth. For amusement, trust, and knowing to exist, fear does not have to be completely eradicated. In fact, it can't be. It's perfectly acceptable and normal to feel fearful *and* amused, scared *and* trusting. That's part of being human. We have complex emotions and experiences, and it is rarely black and white.

CHAPTER 24
ONE OF THESE THINGS IS NOT LIKE THE OTHER (AND THAT'S OKAY)

Comparison is a natural human skill, and we learn it at an early age, as part of sorting and grouping identical or similar things. A picture of all red shapes and we say the green one doesn't belong. An assortment of fruits and we say the potato doesn't fit with the group. A friend of mine refers to humans as "lazy thinkers," meaning that our brains are structured to look for the easy way out in defining things. In many areas of development, this is a skill that serves us quite well (we can sort rotten blueberries from fresh ones, for example). My sister has her doctorate in human development and has spent years doing math research with preschoolers. I am in love with her stories of kiddos' perception and candid feedback.

So where does comparison hold us back sometimes? In certain social settings. And this is one of the biggest discussions around challenges with social media. We compare our lives and selves to what people make visible on a screen, and it's not only usually unrealistic, it's irrelevant. But we forget that. We often start to think that there's something wrong with us, something damaged because the nightstand by our bed looks like a book avalanche rather than a magazine cover. (I'm actually kind of proud of my book stack. If nothing else, maybe it will show my kids that I value reading as an adult. It certainly shows my love of learning.)

In comparison, there is a fear of not belonging. Of being the potato among apples and pears. Fear of rejection. Fear of loneliness and isolation. I found myself waist-deep, or more honestly neck-deep, in some of this comparing just recently. I was in so far that I almost didn't even see it! Someone I respect greatly just published a book. It was a wonderful idea, it was executed well, and it sold well from the beginning. She seems to be having *all* the homeruns in her business and none of the strikeouts. I made up in my head, I suppose, that she has limitless resources. Especially since I'm in the middle of working on a book myself, I compared myself to her situation immediately. I thought, *She has so much time to work. I have next to none. She has so many ideas and is flying high, and I will never get there.* I didn't see it at the very beginning, but she and I are in completely different seasons of life. Her kids are a good bit older than mine, for instance. And that's only one of the differences, I'm sure.

Birdie Gunyon Meyer, a presenter during my perinatal mental health certificate training, referred to the seasons of life in which we find ourselves. During the postpartum period, she often reminds families that they are in a season of receiving rather than a season of giving and that, while it may not feel comfortable for them to accept, it is a natural time for them to do so; they will have their turn to give later. I absolutely loved her description and have used it with clients and friends more times than I can count (thanks Birdie!). This thought of seasons translates seamlessly to our seasons of growth, with businesses and otherwise. Right now, I am in a season of creativity *and* I'm also raising littles, and as a family we made the choice for me to be a mostly stay-at-home mom.

Are we not all in completely, or mostly, different seasons of life? There is so much that we don't see of other people. There are countless variables, and comparing is impossible. We like to think we can compare to make sense of the world, in the way we could sort cars of the same colors or blocks of the same size when we were younger, but . . . no. We just can't. Comparison can totally zap amusement. Let's zap comparison when it's not needed instead.

CHAPTER 25
YOU BROKE AN AXLE

Were you an Oregon Trail kid? Did you watch that stinking squirrel twitch across the screen while you tried desperately to "shoot" it for your family's dinner? Those darn squirrels. They were always the hardest to get. And the rabbits. You hoped for one of those slow, big animals. Those were easy targets.

For those of you who didn't grow up playing this game of questionable educational value (okay, okay, I'm sure there was value) in your school computer lab, let me clue you in. Oregon Trail was a game in which you attempted, with your family aboard a covered wagon, to travel along the historic Oregon Trail while staying alive and well. One of the things that was always a bummer and that you needed supplies to fix was a broken axle (those pesky trail rocks!). I never broke an axle in real life until . . . well, until we did!

A couple months ago, my husband left for work, driving our 2003 Subaru Forester—or so I thought. Just a few minutes after he left, he walked back in the door, holding in his hand a greasy metal doughnut. (Actually, I texted a picture to our mechanic and he said it looked like a chocolate doughnut. Thanks, Mike. I *think* we should be paying you?) Long story short, the lower control arm on the driver's side had broken, and I guess that put stress on the axle, because that broke too! I will never forget the video I took of the tow truck driver attempting to get the car up lined up to get onto the flatbed. It *almost drove off of its wheel*. I mean, the sight of it all. I couldn't help myself, I just started laughing! In between reassuring our kids that our car would be okay and that it was fine for a stranger to be driving our car, the giggles just would not quit. I'm smiling even as I write this. If I wasn't in public, there may or may not be some audible laughter.

Sparks

    The luck of this happening right outside of our house and not while my husband was actually in the middle of his commute is not lost on us. We are extremely grateful for the timing! And I found that there was absolutely nothing to do but laugh through this. Because we broke an axle. Just like on the Oregon Trail. So when you break your own axle, see if there could be a glimmer of funny. Just a touch—just enough to get out of the heaviness of the moment and see things as they truly are. If you find it, you will enjoy yourself a whole lot more!

CHAPTER 26
MINI MEDITATIONS

Meditation and self-reflection practices come in all shapes and sizes. They are a sure way to help us change how we are seeing something and turn up the volume on amusement. Sometimes the idea of meditating conjures up images of sitting in uncomfortable positions for uncomfortably long periods of time, with an uncomfortable amount of silence. But really, to meditate is just, according to Merriam-Webster.com:
1. "To engage in contemplation or reflection
2. To engage in mental exercise . . . for the purpose of reaching a heightened level of spiritual awareness."

Think of all the possibilities! A reflective practice can easily be something that you tailor to fit *your* needs. It doesn't have to look or sound or feel just one way. After my daughter was born, I needed something that was easily accessible. My spirit needed some nourishment, but I didn't have the time or focus to sit for long (or short) periods of time to meditate. Besides, it wasn't what my soul was asking for anyway. It wanted something different.

I was introduced to oracle cards by our doula during my first pregnancy, and I totally gave her the side eye the first time she pulled them out. I wasn't fully owning my "woo" side then, and I really had no idea what they were, how to use them, or how they fit into my life. But before long, I fell in love with the simple magic of picking the "right" card every time and reading the message it had for me. Using them as inspiration for some meditative time has been one of the most accessible ways to remain connected to my spirituality during times of stress or even just busyness. I also reach for the decks during times of joy. They have a wonderful grounding quality about them.

Depending on the deck you are working with, the messages you receive will have different themes. For example, I have a beloved deck called the *Mother's Wisdom Deck* by Niki Dewart and Elizabeth Marglin (unfortunately no longer available), and naturally all of the guidance connected to the cards relates back to one's parenting journey and relationship with their children. It might offer information about a behavior we are doing or not doing, or an opportunity to approach a situation with a new perspective. You can draw one card at a time or draw several. Many decks come with a guidebook that walks you through how to do different readings. You can also rely on that beautiful gut feeling to guide you. I have loved doing a "year-ahead spread" of cards (like on the Wild Unknown blog) at the beginning of or right before a new year. It's such an interesting way of looking at themes for the coming months and can be something neat to reflect on as you move through your year.

Oracle Decks in Action

When my second child was an infant, I had a nightly ritual. I would get cozy in some pajama pants, make sure I had on a nursing-friendly shirt (because of course she would require a snack before bed), and pop my daughter into our well-loved, gray Ergo. In my darkened bedroom, we would start to *shhh*, sway, and rock. I would find my way over to my dresser, which had belonged to my grandmother, and let my hands find the deck of cards.

Feeling my feet planted firmly on the ground, I would "shuffle" the deck (I still haven't mastered that beautiful arching card trick) and hold it to my daughter's back, as close to my heart as I could get. Breathing deeply, I would ask for guidance, either generally or around something specific. At the time, my questions often had to do with my role as a mother. Our family's flow, with adding a second little to the mix, was going through a time of great transition. I regularly worried about whether I was the mother my family needed and whether I was mothering well.

What I would get from the cards, without fail, was always exactly what I needed. Sometimes the card was so clearly linked to a present-day challenge or question that it might as well have smacked me in the face. Sometimes the message wouldn't be clear to me right away, and I would leave the card on the dresser for a few days to let the message sink in.

And unsurprisingly, it always did. Something that continues to amaze me is when I draw a particular card time and time again. Clearly, it's begging for attention to a certain theme in my life.

There was a period of time between having my son and daughter when I kept pulling the "snake" card from my *Mother's Wisdom Deck*. Again and again and again. There was no way I could ignore it. The card speaks to connecting to the things that energize us and enlighten us to things that could be getting in the way of connecting with that energy. There were plenty of times when I felt spent after having my son, and this card was one thing that kept turning my attention back to that—to the fact that I was worthy of that attention.

As my daughter got older, I shifted away from the nighttime card meditation. I don't remember exactly when things changed, or why. The cards haven't gone anywhere, though, and I now have three beloved decks. Each feels right to use at different times. I'm so grateful for the roots of all of the varying messages from different cultures and traditions reflected in the cards and their accompanying guidebooks, and how easily the messages are translated into present-day life. It's beautiful. They remind me not only to get out of my own head, but that something other than fear truly *is* driving. (See the Resources for some card decks that I recommend!)

CHAPTER 27
"I BELIEVE IN YOU, BUT I'M NOT AFRAID OF YOU"

Last night, we chose to have a picnic dinner on the floor while watching a movie. After the prior couple of weeks (husband and both kids with the flu, sick dog requiring inpatient hydration and meds, follow-up ear infection and 24-hour virus for one little one), it was exactly what we needed: Indian takeout in front of the TV and *Guardians of the Galaxy*. The movie was definitely advanced for my kids, but we made a point of talking about challenging themes and explaining things that might be confusing or upsetting.

To be honest, I was getting up and down a fair amount during the movie. It wasn't my most beautiful display of being in the moment! We had mountains of laundry piling up in the laundry room, and it felt good to me to be working through some of that. What absolutely caught my ear and eyes, though, was the villain, Pitch Black. It's funny how working on this book has made things stand out, almost as if they were highlighted for me. In the movie, Pitch's character was responsible for creating nightmares and he claimed to be (and boasted about being) intimately familiar with everyone's worst fear. He wanted to be known for his powers and sinister role, but all of the guardians (interestingly, religious holiday-related characters such as Santa and the Easter Bunny are included along with the Tooth Fairy, Jack Frost, and the Sand Man) aimed to defeat him and protect the children of the world from his darkness.

At the part where the guardians rise against Pitch Black, they realize they need the help of some of the children; they can't do it on their own. One little boy says such a wise thing to Pitch: "I do believe in you. I'm just not afraid of you." Ah! My excitement when I heard this! The kids didn't need from protection from that fear! What they needed was a mindset shift about how they regarded it. Pitch couldn't hurt them, after all. The movie (I hope I'm not spoiling this for anyone) has a beautifully surprising ending in which Pitch Black ends up having fears himself, and they end up destroying him.

We know that fear is real. Of course it is. We feel it, we live it, we know it. We also know that it doesn't have to have absolute power. It doesn't have to control our actions and lives. We have a choice where we can stand up to it and say, "Sure, I see you. I feel you. And I'm not going to let that hold me back." I absolutely loved how this was shown, and with a kiddo no less, in the movie.

Exercise Idea

Watch *Guardians of the Galaxy*. See what themes about fear stand out to you and how they might be inspiration for working through your own.

CHAPTER 28
GRATITUDE

I would be absolutely missing something if I didn't at least touch on gratitude here. When working as a therapist I, like many other mental health providers, often assign a gratitude journal to my clients in order to help shift their mindset. I would explain to them that practicing gratitude, even if you feel like you're faking it in the beginning, leads to actually feeling grateful. (Yes, there is research behind this. See the Resources section for more information!) Every time I've kept a gratitude journal, which is really just a list, I have experienced a shift in perspective. It's sometimes more gradual than others, but it is always there. I might be feeling down on myself, unsure of what I really have going for me, but when I start to actually keep track of the great things in my life, big or small, I really start to appreciate them.

Sometimes, when you start your list, the things on it might not seem particularly inspired or inspiring. *Toenail clippers. Garbage disposals. Ear hair trimmers.* But before long, you will likely start surprising yourself by even looking out for things to add to your list during the day. And how cool to be able to spot things for which you're grateful *in the moment* when you're experiencing them!

Just this morning, I watched a recording of former monk, speaker, and podcaster Jay Shetty on *The Ellen DeGeneres Show* talking about planting seeds as an analogy for practicing gratitude. Jay talks about "planting" seeds of gratitude in your life so that they will grow and take up space instead of the "weeds" of anger, worry, fear, and so forth. What a beautiful image! I have heard of thinking of our minds as a garden before, and envisioning taking out the dead plants and overgrowth to make room for healthy plants, but I like the idea of using it specifically with gratitude. Because if we plant the seeds, they will grow. That's the gorgeous thing.

Sparks

It might feel inauthentic at first, but before you know it, it will turn into a full-blown authentic, magical forest of gratitude ferns and faeries. Lots less room for all of the fear-inducing crud we talked about in Part One.

Exercise Idea

Gratitude seeds aren't the only kind we can plant throughout our day! Maybe start with one type, like gratitude, and then experiment with other types of seeds as well. Think about planting amusement seeds. Trust seeds. Knowing seeds! What kinds would yours be? Vegetables? Flowers? Where would you sprinkle them throughout your day?

PART THREE
KNOWING, TRUST, AND OTHER FUN

Quiet. Space. Me. When I started on my adventure with the year-long intuitive training course, I was not just committing to completing it and learning the material, I was agreeing to find space for myself each week so I could keep current with what was being taught.

Sitting on a wooden dining room chair; on the soft and comfortable, yet peeling chair in my office; or on my bedroom floor, I became grounded almost at the very sound of her voice. My teacher, Stacia, pre-recorded our weekly classes so we could complete them when it worked for us.

Most days, the only time I could find was after the kids' bedtime. I found a darkened space to settle in and be guided by Stacia for the week's exercise. It wasn't uncommon for me to be interrupted by a cry or request to nurse; this was a need I could easily meet and then return to my solitude. More quickly than I could have anticipated, I dropped into the weekly meditations. My spirit seemed familiar with them, even though much of the content was new to me.

I've referred to this feeling elsewhere as well, but settling into my intuition and becoming familiar with it felt like a homecoming. I imagine sometimes that the Universe must have been frustrated with my inability to consistently tune into my inner knowing earlier in my life. I think that must be a voice from within me, though. It's hard to imagine that the Universe would be anything but patient, kind, and full of love for where we find ourselves on our journeys.

CHAPTER 29
INTUITION AND KNOWING

Intuition is somewhat of a buzzword these days. Maybe it's the people I surround myself with, but I feel as though the word is popping up almost everywhere. That's a great thing because it's getting talked about. It's getting experimented with and lived and breathed. For the purposes of this book, though, I want to call it something different. So, if intuition is your deep inner knowing, I'm going to refer to knowing.

Here's what I mean by knowing:
- Your gut feeling
- Your inner voice (not the critic, but the one that speaks with love and compassion)
- Your "Spidey sense"
- A feeling of calm and acceptance

One of the most valuable things that I learned through my intuition course is that everyone has access to this knowing. Just like with any skill, some may naturally have greater ease with certain aspects of it, but also like with other skills, practicing it and learning about it make it more accessible and usable.

Exercise Idea
Think of a time when you felt that inner knowing. Did you listen to it? What was it trying to tell you? Start to become aware of this tug at your consciousness. It's usually a calm voice, not a panicked one. Be cautious about confusing your knowing voice with your what-if fear voice. With practice, it gets easier to discern the difference between the two. The biggest thing: don't judge yourself when it's hard to tell the difference. Again, we're human and figuring out this life in these bodies. It's not always straightforward, and we get chances to try again.

CHAPTER 30
OWNING MY KNOWING

When I was in my early 20s, my therapist suggested that I see an intuitive counselor to supplement the work I was doing in therapy. My therapist knew I had a huge interest in spirituality and thought that connecting with a like-minded practitioner might be helpful for me. I scheduled an appointment, curious and excited.

While making an audio recording of the session, the counselor channeled some of my relatives who had passed on and she also looked into some of my past lives. She used this information to provide clues as to what I might be experiencing in my then-current life, relaying the information with compassion and gentleness. She is the first intuitive person I had heard talk about free will, and how she was not comfortable "telling the future" because what she might see was only one outcome of many possible futures. As humans, we are given free will and can change the course of our lives, thereby changing the future.

Cognitively I maintained a somewhat-hesitant stance about the whole process, but I found it impossible to ignore my physical and emotional response to the content of the session. Everything felt so aligned. I felt so calm and connected during and after my time there. My thoughts hadn't quite settled, though. I kept wondering all sorts of things: *How can any of this be true? What if it's not? What if that woman was totally tricking me?*

At some point, even if years down the road, I decided that I didn't need to get caught up in all those thoughts. I didn't need to know 100 percent of why she was able to do the intuitive work and whether it was based in reality. All I needed to know were what these things brought up for me, that it felt right, and that it started me on a great deal of spiritual growth.

Sparks

I never went back to see that first intuitive counselor. I felt like I had gotten what I needed at the time, and I didn't have the resources to make seeing her a regular thing. It was another year or two before I found myself seeking guidance from another similar type of healer.

I met her at a local meditation group she led, and I had several sessions with her. Using Reiki and intuition, she guided me through healing several blockages and old stories I had been carrying with me. This relationship was one that was very powerful for me. I received a great deal of spiritual nurturing, and it was exactly what I needed at the time. Unfortunately, things became quite confusing to me when seeing both my therapist and spiritual counselor at the same time began to feel like a conflict. It was then that I released a great deal of my spiritual connectedness. I pushed it away, locked it up, and didn't necessarily have plans to open the door again.

But here's the problem with that: That door didn't want to stay closed. Have you ever had a door with a magnetic latch and it just keeps popping back open? Push. *Pop*. Push. *Pop*. This was kind of like that.

Again and again, spirituality and knowing kept showing up in my life. And I missed them terribly when they weren't regular parts of my day. It was like that flame that we've been talking about wasn't being fed. When you keep getting the call, you will eventually answer. I kept putting the calls on hold: *I'm sorry, Emily isn't available right now, but check back in with her in a few months to a year and she'll consider chatting with you then.*

Time after time, from multiple sources, I received messages that I was meant to use knowing and spirituality in my work and life. Finally, I began to pick up the calls and engage. First, my engagement was tentative. The original fear of worrying what people thought about me being "out there" faded bit by bit (not my business anyway!). I hadn't wanted to be seen as a spacey or woo, but at some point being seen as however I would be seen if I was being myself felt way less scary than stuffing my realness away. I am a professional *and* value spirituality and intuition. I can be both. (Mind blown).

One of the cool things with how Stacia teaches about intuition and knowing is that they're not some exclusive thing. To be sure, some people have an easier time than others gleaning certain skills, but isn't that life? With practice, we are all able to start tuning into the part of us that knows.

The voice of inner knowing isn't critical. It's not that inner dialogue that shames you or tells you how much you suck. Your voice of knowing is steady, compassionate, and loving.

Say what? My inner voice doesn't sound like that.

Breathe easy. It's only because you might not have listened to your knowing in a bit. Your inner critic might be so loud that it's drowning out your knowing. That happens. Even when you've got lots of practice under your belt, that still happens from time to time. Again, knowing which voice is which, and practicing that discernment, will help you to be able to remind fear or your critic to step down.

Fine-tuning your awareness of your knowing does take time, and there is no one right path to take. When do you feel that peaceful quiet? Nature? While doing art? When listening to music? Those are good places to start. When you first start listening, you might notice that your inner critic is super loud and is telling you how stupid all of this is. Gently remind them that you've got this under control, and that while they can be there, they will need to turn down their volume.

Exercise Idea

Decide on your place of peaceful quiet. Go there at least once this week. Maybe bring some paper and jot down what thoughts enter your mind. Don't think too much about what to write; just let it flow. What comes through?

CHAPTER 31
USING YOUR KNOWING TO MEET YOUR INNER CHILD

My son looks at me, his eyes so big, brown, and beautiful. They're questioning and full of uncertainty, and something inside of me clicks. I see me. Gulp. That is for sure one looking glass I do *not* want to look into.

My son's introduction to preschool has been a process. There have been tears and fretting, long snuggle sessions, and space for processing this huge change. It has required a ton of patience and—as much as I wish I had remembered to anticipate this ahead of time—self-reflection. In holding space for my son's big feelings, there have been countless moments when I have forgotten to acknowledge my own.

There is something about the way emotions show up in our kids that acts as a flawless mirror for what is behind the scenes in our own bodies and minds. Littles are plugged in to us. It's no wonder we feel so deeply when they feel. It's not only because they own such a large piece of real estate in our hearts, it's because it awakens—especially in us empaths—memories, sensations, and all sorts of feelings we might not be conscious of.

To revisit Part One, I had my own separation anxieties as a kid. I had intense fear about being away from my parents, especially in kindergarten. For me, it was mainly focused on the school environment too. I internalized many of my worries, quietly crying and listening to my thoughts in my head rather than voicing them out loud. My teacher told me eventually that she didn't want me to ask for reassurance anymore, as I had sought it so frequently. I can't blame her for setting that boundary given her other responsibilities, but it's not what I needed at the time. My fears surfaced in other areas throughout my childhood and adolescence, but this seems to be where they are rooted.

What became super clear at some point after the start of my son's preschool year was that my internal reaction (both emotional and physical) to my son's fears was only partly due to my discomfort with seeing my son in distress. The other part was a younger version of me, reflected from what I was seeing in my son, tugging on my shirt and whispering her fears.

Psst. I'm here. Am I safe?

A direct communication needed to happen. I needed to say hello to the little girl inside and let her know she was okay. I needed to pause and give myself some of the patience and compassion I had been showing my sweet son. Because, inside of me, there is a sweet little girl too. This was a powerful exercise in "what's mine is mine." In order to be fully present for my son, I needed to own my "stuff" and separate it from his. I could notice the difference between what was mine to process and what was my compassion bubbling up for my boy. That way, I could identify that the acid in my stomach and part of the tug on my emotions were mine to address at a different time, not in that moment. And wow, does that have an impact. Showing up for our kids is everything, but showing up for our inner children is important, too. In fact, identifying these personal reactions to current situations is exactly what allows us to be present with our kids when they're navigating their "stuff."

* * *

"After this one sleep, I'm going to school?"

These days, this question doesn't have as much of a pull on me as it used to. But months ago, it started a chain reaction that began as an ache in my heart and quickly moved to burning in my stomach. A churning, uncomfortable feeling. The kind of feeling you want to push away. The kind of feeling that persists if you resist. (And—oops—I resisted more times than I would like to admit!) The good news is if we pause to check in with our knowing, and wonder why something feels so strong for us, there is often some important information underneath.

Exercise Idea

How do we figure out when an emotional reaction includes information for us, or whether it's a reaction to the current situation alone?

1. Pause and check in. Especially if you notice that your reaction is stronger than the situation warrants, take some space. Get honest with yourself. Do some journaling, meditate, have a quick chat with yourself. This is helpful even if you're reacting only to what your child is feeling. Taking some space is great for gaining perspective.
2. Identify which emotions you're experiencing and what they want to say. Example: *I'm feeling fear. It wants to make sure everyone is safe. It wants to tell me something feels scary.*
3. Take note of who is feeling the emotion. Current you? Five-year-old you? Fifteen-year-old you? Many times a much-younger version of us can be looking for reassurance. Just get curious and put judgment aside.
4. Release. Through more journaling, writing a letter to the version of yourself with the emotion, visualizations, and so forth, let your part go.

CHAPTER 32
TRUST

As we move away from fear, there is something that is asked of us. It's something that can be so hard when we're facing the unknown: trust.

It's one thing to have trust issues in relationships and even with yourself, but have you thought about whether you have trust issues with the Universe or with whichever higher power is within your belief system? I have, and some days they still pop up.

At times in my life I've lost faith that things would feel better or get better, especially when I was feeling extremely anxious or depressed. After the birth of my son, even as a therapist who logically "knew better," I wondered whether I would feel like a sleepless ball of nerves for the rest of motherhood. It's scary to not know. I felt betrayed by the Universe. I felt almost that I was owed a perfect transition to parenthood since I had experienced such an uncomfortable pregnancy. Silly, right? There it was anyway.

When it comes to trusting the Universe, we usually want the signs and validation to conform to the way *we* think things should be. We want our manifestations to occur exactly how *we* painted them, on a time line that *we* decided. Sometimes, this does happen! That's pretty magical. More often, though, things look different than we ever could have imagined. This doesn't mean they're less powerful or magical, and often they're even more so. There is no way to determine this ahead of time, so what needs to be in place is trust. Trust that things will work out, one way or another. Trust that we are going to get where we need and want to go.

To get to trust we need to let go of control. And to tell you the truth, it's more letting go of the *idea* of control, because we never really had it in the first place. This is equally terrifying and freeing at the same time. Feel into it.

Exercise Idea

Do you feel trust in yourself? What about the Universe (or God, Source, etc.)? Make a list of all the times you have come through for yourself and surprised yourself or others with your skill or capability. Do the same for the Universe. When has it come through for you and provided just wanted you needed?

CHAPTER 33
RELEASING DOUBT AND TRUSTING YOURSELF

I believe you know her well, as I do.

She can be sneaky, dipping in and out, then swinging out from her hiding place when we least expect her, surprising the heck out of us. She's the voice questioning launching a business versus remaining at a job that makes us feel inauthentic and empty. She's the one asking if we can be really certain that our actions are a good idea. Essentially, she always says, "Oh I don't know if you should do that. That seems . . . *risky*."

Do you know her name? We don't always speak it. It's doubt. And she is related to fear! She definitely takes on the fear of something happening/not happening vibe, or fear of not being good enough.

I have often heard clients question their actions even *before* they've taken action. It's no secret (although sometimes it feels like one) that we all have doubts. We second-guess ourselves and have an inner part tugging at us to be safe, secure, and predictable. Because what could happen? Have you ever heard the doubt voice, realized it made a good point, and decided to slip back into familiarity so you didn't have to hear it again? I have.

Doubt is a function of the part of our minds that wants to keep us safe. And as humans, we know that in order to succeed we have to be comfortable with a certain degree of *discomfort*. That doesn't mean that we make the decision move past doubt once and we're done. It's something that flows as our lives do.

Some people have the tendency toward doubt to a greater degree, but that doesn't mean they can't be effective in their lives. It just means that there is a need for an even stronger commitment to building and practicing insight, awareness, and skills.

Doubt is pervasive. We wonder about our parenting decisions. *Did I choose the right school? Right bedtime? Right snack?* We wonder about our business choices. *Is what I'm doing with my career the right choice for our family? Is it responsible to start my own business? Am I capable of meeting my clients' needs? Will I earn enough money to help support my kids? Will people like what I'm offering?* We can work with these thoughts.

Doubt likely won't magically disappear from your inner dialogue. Since it serves a function (keeping us safe), it can offer an important different perspective to consider. Let's not let her steal the show, though! Trust in yourself. Trust in your world. When we allow for trust, we allow for amusement. Your knowing will also help guide you.

Here are three ways to put doubt in her place.

1. Talk to her with compassion. *Oh hey, doubt. No wonder you're scared. This is a big step. And you know what? I've got this. We're going to be okay.*
2. Make a trust journal. Each day, list five reasons you can trust yourself. Things could be *I know how to communicate with clients* or *I have good speaking skills* or *I am resourceful.*
3. Do something that pushes you outside of your safety zone a few times each week. On purpose! Think about writing a blog post that shares a bit more of you, trying a new marketing angle, or even experimenting with a new recipe.

CHAPTER 34
LEANING INTO TRUST AND TAKING YOUR TIME

> "Trust is our antidote to fear. It aligns us with the flow of life—a magnificent energy that guides and directs us so that we can live expansive, happy, and fulfilling lives."
> ~ Gillian Anderson and Jennifer Nadel, *We: A Manifesto for Women Everywhere*

The fear of not enough time—to get things done, to have the chance to experience this lifetime with loved ones, to see the world—impacts us when we're trying our best to be present in our lives and learn about why we're here. As I write this book, I often wonder when I'll have a chunk of time long enough to really move this thing forward.

This is where trust comes in. And intentions and dedication. *I will not abandon this idea. I will not leave it. I will keep coming back and keep coming back. I will just write. I might have a slower time line, but that's just building a more solid relationship with this book. I'm getting to know it and allowing it to gain breath and life.*

The taking my time reminds me of when I met my husband (who just brought me a slice of gluten-free pizza because he knows I'm in a creative "zone" and he said he wants to make sure I get fed!). We didn't really move into our relationship super-fast. Don't get me wrong: There was an early connection and intention to spend a great deal of time together, but there was also a building of a deeper friendship. Our relationship gained life and breath. Had we skipped that part, I suspect we wouldn't have the lasting goofiness and resilience that we do.

We both had to trust that the other was committed to this thing going the distance. Our words and actions were there, sure, but there is a bigger, overarching trust of "You see me. You get me. You love me anyway and you're here." We can have that same exchange with the life we're living, with how we trust God or the Universe to show up for us.

Exercise Idea

What things are you worried you won't have enough time to do? Make a list. Get those things out of your head! What is the most important *right now*? What steps can you take to accomplish it if it's important, or let it go if it doesn't truly serve you?

CHAPTER 35
COMPASSION

We can be so freaking hard on ourselves. I don't need to tell you that; it's not news to you. Our inner voices can be critical, hateful, and harsh. There is another way.

We can start to train ourselves to lead with compassion. A compassion-filled mindset seamlessly lends itself to amusement, knowing, and trust. When you're not resisting *you*, you are so much more open to all the world has to offer. Just like most other things I have written about, compassion takes practice. We might consider ourselves to be compassionate people, but turn your attention to your inner life. How compassionate is that inner experience? How often do you give yourself the same grace you give others in the world?

It can help to see your situation from the outside. So take a moment to distance yourself from your experience, just enough so you can see the facts and the full picture. See yourself sitting there, the situation unfolding as if you were an onlooker. Notice, and imagine what you might say differently to this person experiencing life. How might you speak to them differently?

Lean in. Notice. Set judgment aside.

Exercise Idea
Actually answer the questions in this chapter! Make a practice of speaking to yourself gently.

CHAPTER 36
AUTHENTICITY AND SELF-CARE

When we're given the opportunity to express ourselves in complete comfort and are able to live a life that aligns with our values and what we know fills us, we experience an ignition of our inner fire that makes us feel unstoppable. It is the pinnacle of self-truth, and of knowing ourselves. This is a matter of privilege as well. Many don't get to live into their full authentic selves because of the color of their skin, who they love, or their religious practices. And just to be clear, that is bullshit. Getting to be who we are, while having compassion for others, is a human right.

For years, a recurring subject in my own therapy sessions was my discomfort with appearing inauthentic. I didn't like faking feeling one way when I felt the opposite, or doing something just because I "had" to or it was expected of me. It seemed I was fearful of losing myself; I didn't want to get confused and lose track of whom I was and where I was going. It's interesting that I thought that could happen. In addition to that discomfort, it also became very clear to me over the years that authenticity is simply one of my biggest values. I want it front and center.

When I decided to make the shift from offering therapy to offering coaching, I wanted a title that would set me apart from other coaches in a world of what seems like thousands of coaches. I knew that it would have to be something that felt aligned with my sense of self and my values, and that it would click for me when I heard it or said it. I landed on "self-care and authenticity coach" because it felt like exactly the way I want to help people advance in their lives. Though that's not the title I currently use, authenticity will always be one of my central values.

In the name of authenticity, I will share that as I type this, my almost-2-year-old daughter is switching between putting her foot on the side of my face and lacing my hair through her toes, and tapping the laptop keyboard with her foot. And pulling my hair. As much as I want to just be grateful for that tiny foot and that tiny hand in this moment, it's hard. I'm touched out. After a day of being climbed on (and yes, kissed and hugged too), my body is screaming for space. What's underlying that immense need? *Oh hey, fear. What's up?* Fear that I won't be able to stand it if I get touched one more time. Fear of not finishing this book. *Fear that my needs won't be met.*

Now that I have made that initial realization, I can choose to shift my perspective. For example, I can choose compassion for myself. Of course I'm annoyed. Of course I'm short-tempered. It's the end of the day and more than anything I just want some space to write. And instead, my daughter won't sleep. So while I *am* writing, my attention is divided.

That brings me to self-care. It is absolutely essential for us to be in a place of having our needs met, at least to some extent, in order to be as open as possible to amusement, knowing, and trust. And to be the healthiest version of ourselves! When we are not taking care of even our basic needs (sleep, nourishment, space), we start to close off and hunker down rather than open up. For me, self-care looks like securing several hours each week to write and take care of other business-related tasks. Or just to sit, uninterrupted with a cup of tea and a book. And that's just what part of my care looks like. Yours, as it was with joy, will look completely different. Not to mention, we all have different pockets of time and different resources. Either way, caring for yourself fuels your fire. It creates sparks, which all at once can come together with others and burst into flame.

CHAPTER 37
GENEROSITY

Have you noticed a theme of openness throughout Part Two and Part Three? Being open primes us to be positioned to receive life from a place of amusement and to actively engage with our knowing and trust.

One of the things fear can cause us to do is to close off in an attempt to "protect" our resources (whether time, money, etc.) with the belief that they are limited and scarce. There will be seasons when we are able to be generous with different resources that are available to us, but we always have a chance to be generous with something.

Generosity is an opening—an allowing of flow. When we let things flow out of our lives, we can also let things flow back in. This can feel really tough. I have for sure had some barricaded, triple-bolted doors around me before, especially when it comes to financial resources. I felt super-scared that we were running out—that we wouldn't have enough. And guess what? Somehow we've always been okay.

During those times, I have needed to keep after myself to unbolt the doors and crack them open. Because even if I don't have extra income to spare, I have the ability to be generous with compliments, or maybe my time, advice, or skills. I can watch your kiddo while you run to the store. I can bring soup when you're sick. We can practice generosity in so many ways. I will note, though, that after reading *It's Not Your Money* by Tosha Silver, I experienced the power of keeping money flowing in my life and being generous with it, even if it's $10, $5, or $1.

Practicing generosity doesn't only give the receiver something; it gives the giver something as well. It allows the giver to participate in the flow and feel good through providing. Remember that there are seasons in our lives when we're in full receiver mode, and that's okay. But notice whether you're in that place. If not, in what small ways can you start to share? Another note on sharing: take care not to be so generous that you're feeling depleted, because that pretty much defeats the purpose. That's why I'm focusing on small steps here. Find your personal "sweet spot"—how much you feel comfortable giving. This will fluctuate and shift depending on what else is going on in your life.

Exercise Idea

Make a list of 10 super-simple generosity ideas. Here are some ideas to get you started:

- Double your dinner recipe and surprise a neighbor with a meal
- Drop a note in the mail to a friend, telling them how much you appreciate them and why
- Offer a colleague a complimentary pick-your-brain session
- Round up your purchase amount at the cash register if the store offers the option of donating to a charity

Commit to acting on one of your ideas over the next week. The following week, pick another!

CHAPTER 38
THE ONLY WAY IN IS IN

If the only way out (of fear) is through, the only way to get into amusement, trust, and knowing, is in. If we want to live these things and feel these things, we need to *practice* these things. By practicing, we lean into the possibility of what life could look like if we saw things a bit differently.

Many times when we begin something new, it feels strange. It can feel awkward or unnatural, just like wobbling on a bike when you first learn to ride or driving a car for the first several times. This is to be expected. Avoid shaming yourself and expect it as part of the experience. If you notice judgment of yourself come up, just see it. Regard it from a bit of distance and get curious. What's it telling you? Is it asking for some reassurance or is it a voice of a younger you from long ago? Send it a message that you're going to lean into these skills anyway, and that you're going to do it imperfectly. Just like with any new behavior, all you need to do is keep showing up. Keep trying.

One of the other roadblocks to getting into the flow of amusement and its friends might be whether or not you're giving yourself permission to enjoy life or see things from a new perspective. Do you truly believe that you're deserving? That you are worthy? If you read Part One (and I hope you did, because it's pretty essential!), you know that there can be a journey to shedding some of the stories that keep us in fear. Therapy, coaching, and other practices can support us in moving through.

Exercise Idea
Make a list of things you've tried that you felt so incredibly strange at the beginning. They don't need to be things that you've mastered, but just things that you have experimented with. And make a note of the things at which you've become really skilled; look at how far you've come!

Exercise Idea

In more than one of her books, Brené Brown has written about her practice of writing permission slips. Grant yourself permission to do whatever it is that you are keeping yourself from. It can be feeling a certain way, such as confident or empowered, or doing something, such as taking a class or buying a book you've wanted to read. Write it down and make it official!

I, Emily, give myself permission to write a book that lights me up even though I'm not sure what will come from it!

CHAPTER 39
WELL, THAT'S FUNNY

In working on this book, I moved back and forth between sections and chapters to add to the initial structure with a flow guided by my inner knowing. I noticed at some point that I kept feeling a pull to add to Part One, almost to the point where I was ignoring Part Two and Part Three.

If you've read this far, you know that Part One is all about fear, and Part Two and Part Three are all about amusement, trust, and knowing. Sure, there is some overlap, because we can't very well talk about some of the topics without revisiting fear and defining how to release it. But how ironic is it that while I have been writing this book, I keep being pulled back to fear? It's like it's craving my attention and wants all of my time spent there. I need to clear that up.

Dear Fear: Goodness, I am so sorry, but hanging out is not at all what this project is about. My apologies if you misunderstood. You see, I think you got confused when I gave you such a large amount of attention in Part One. That's totally cool. You're useful for some things, but I've got to tell you: Part Two and Part Three are about learning to release fear's power. So, I'm going to ask that you recognize that and let the process happen. Thanks for what you've done to keep me safe in the past, but I'm all set now.

This is 100 percent a great example of how, even once we've had lots of practice with identifying and releasing stories and patterns that come up in our lives, sometimes they still happen! I have said it one million times before and will say it again: That's because we're human. We can have compassion for our imperfect humanness and know that this is just kind of how we were built. We're not robots; we are wired in a much different way.

I am so excited to have uncovered what was happening with the pull between the two sections. It's like I didn't want to leave Part One behind or hurt its feelings. Wow. If anthropromorphizing is attributing human emotions to animals, is there such a thing as bibliomorphizing? Because I think I'm guilty of that.

Now that we've cleared that out of the way, let's finish strong, shall we? It's completely expected that fear will pop here and there, because that's simply the nature of things. Let's work together to remind it what this book's about, gently and without pushing, so that we can focus on the task at hand.

Exercise Idea

How about writing a little love note or letter to your own fear when it pops up for you? You can even do it in your head or out loud. There's really no need to be angry with fear; it's doing its job and that's something I'm thankful for. Even the things that don't serve us well right now or all the time have served a useful function at some point.

Personally, I really enjoy using humor when I do things like this. It helps keep things light and keeps the situation from feeling overwhelming or like a catastrophe. Feel whatever seems right for your specific situation.

CONCLUSION

I can't say this enough. I'm human. You're human. We will both fall out of our mindset shifts. It's absolutely normal to need reminders, practice, and new shifts for new circumstances. If you can expect that, you can find ways to accept that in a nonjudgmental way. As we grow, we will flow in and out of our days, figuring it out. Some days we will totally feel like we've got it down, like we're rocking it and the days when we weren't feel so long ago. On other days, we might feel embarrassed that we reacted the way we did. We will all but forget to be aware of our thoughts and lens. Maybe we snap or yell at our kids, are short with a coworker, or totally flake on a commitment. The key is to aim to not let that throw you (oh, and by the way, that might happen too!) because there is always room for recovery and a different action the next time. We might even be able to shift a moment after our initial reaction by coming out of our autopilot state. We can even regard those hard/rough/icky days with amusement, if we let it into our space. Here's one more example to take with you!

You're walking along on the most beautiful, blue-sky, sunny day. You feel good. And then you smell something. Something not good. Something like poop. And before long, you realize that not only is it, in fact, poop, but it's poop on your shoe. And you're pissed. So. Unbelievably. Angry. Your first thought is: WTAF???!! *Who doesn't clean up after their dog? I'm going to find them, make them smell this awfulness, and have them take me to the shoe store.*

Ready? Here's the opportunity for the shift.

Wow. This. This is kind of silly and it sucks. And on this gorgeous day, I'm getting totally derailed by something that came out of an animal's butt. I'm angry—no wonder I'm angry—and I'm going to choose amusement. Because I get to. I didn't get to choose what I got on my shoe, but I get to choose that.

Sparks

You get to choose! Do not, for a minute, forget that. You have the ability to pause and take stock of the situation to decide what to do next. It takes practice, but lots of things take practice and you've practiced things before (remember that once, long ago, you didn't know how to walk or brush your teeth or rub your belly while patting your head). You absolutely, without a doubt, can open up to amusement, knowing, and trust. Clean those shoes off. Move on with your day.

Can I tell you how excited I am that you are here, reading this paragraph? I love that you're doing the hard stuff (or even just *thinking* about doing the hard stuff), putting yourself out there, and trying something new. You are going to do a great job, and that can include messing up and starting over!

I want to hear your stories! Find me at nestingspacellc@gmail.com and www.nestingspacellc.com.

Remember: feed your sparks. Give them love each day, knowing that they will fuel you. They *are* you.

RESOURCES

Tools for Leaning into Amusement, Knowing, and Trust

Yoga Nidra Network (Includes free recordings)
https://www.yoganidranetwork.org

Gina Sager (yoga nidra recordings for purchase)
https://www.ginasager.com

WooVersity with Stacia Synnestvedt (Intuitive Training and Self-Healing Course, as well as other trainings)
https://www.wooversity.com

Kuan Yin Oracle Deck, Alana Fairchild

Native Spirit Oracle Deck, Denise Linn

Note: More than once, I have been asked about the difference between oracle cards and Tarot cards. I usually think of the term *oracle cards* as an umbrella term that describes cards to be drawn for spiritual guidance or reflection, Tarot being a specific and well-known type. A friend experienced with Tarot sees those cards as having more detailed interpretations and structure. With that said, I have some decks that have extensive entries in the companion guidebook that go along with the cards. So, it might just depend!

Loneliness Research
Human Resources & Services Administration, "The 'Loneliness Epidemic'": https://www.hrsa.gov/enews/past-issues/2019/january-17/loneliness-epidemic

"The Surprising Effects of Loneliness on Health" by Jane E. Brody
https://www.nytimes.com/2017/12/11/well/mind/how-loneliness-affects-our-health.html

Gratitude Research
Giving Thanks Can Make You Happier
https://www.health.harvard.edu/healthbeat/giving-thanks-can-make-you-happier

How Gratitude Changes Your Brain by Joel Wong and Joshua Brown
https://greatergood.berkeley.edu/article/item/how_gratitude_changes_you_and_your_brain

Books
Big Magic: Creative Living Beyond Fear by Elizabeth Gilbert

Dare to Lead: Brave Work. Tough Conversations. Whole Hearts. by Brené Brown

Daring Greatly: How the Courage to Be Vulnerable Transforms the Way We Live, Love, Parent, and Lead by Brené Brown

Fear: Essential Wisdom for Getting Through the Storm by Thich Nhat Hanh

It's Not Your Money: How to Live Fully from Divine Abundance by Tosha Silver

The Brave Learner: Finding Everyday Magic in Homeschool, Learning, and Life by Julie Bogart

The Untethered Soul: The Journey Beyond Yourself by Michael A. Singer

Resources

We: A Manifesto for Women Everywhere by Gillian Anderson and Jennifer Nadel

You are a Badass: How to Stop Doubting Your Greatness and Start Living an Awesome Life by Jen Sincero

You are a Badass at Making Money: Master the Mindset of Wealth by Jen Sincero

Videos
"Developing a Growth Mindset with Carol Dweck" on the Stanford Alumni YouTube channel
https://www.youtube.com/watch?v=hiiEeMN7vbQ

"Ellen Meets Motivational Speaker Jay Shetty" on YouTube
https://www.youtube.com/watch?v=kCb-b0IVCic

"How to Achieve Ultra High Performance: Dr. Michael Gervais on Impact Theory" on YouTube
https://www.youtube.com/watch?v=TYudsPrEGjg

ABOUT THE AUTHOR

Emily Souder is a coach, licensed therapist, and Reiki master practitioner who lives outside of Baltimore, Maryland. She has two adventurous young children and is married to her best friend, who supports her projects and embraces her imperfections. Emily is a lover of laughter, tea, and doing deep personal work. She has authored three books in addition to *Sparks: Birth Story Brave*, *Birth Story Held*, and *Cultivating Amusement*.

www.ingramcontent.com/pod-product-compliance
Lightning Source LLC
Chambersburg PA
CBHW071358080526
44587CB00017B/3122